Freewheeling Through Ireland

ALSO BY EDWARD ENFIELD
FROM CLIPPER LARGE PRINT

Greece on my Wheels

Freewheeling Through Ireland

Enfield Pedals the West Coast

Edward Enfield

W F HOWES LTD

This large print edition published in 2006 by
W F Howes Ltd
Unit 4, Rearsby Business Park, Gaddesby Lane,
Rearsby, Leicester LE7 4YH

1 3 5 7 9 10 8 6 4 2

First published in the United Kingdom in 2006
by Summersdale Publishers Ltd

A CIP catalogue record for this book is available
from the British Library

ISBN 1 84632 437 8

Typeset by Palimpsest Book Production Limited,
Polmont, Stirlingshire
Printed and bound in Great Britain
by Antony Rowe Ltd, Chippenham, Wilts.

CONTENTS

PREFACE   vii

FROM CORK TO GALWAY   1

INTERLUDE – SOME PRELIMINARY
ENCOUNTERS WITH THE IRISH   75

THE SECOND TRIP – CLARE
AND GALWAY   97

MAYO   141

SLIGO AND DONEGAL   173

DUBLIN   200

KERRY AND CORK   215

BIBLIOGRAPHY   243

PREFACE

This book is about my experiences on my bicycle in Ireland, and where it seemed appropriate I have included some passages of Irish history. I ought to follow the usual practice and express my thanks to various learned persons who kindly read the draft and removed a number of errors, but unfortunately I knew no such learned persons whom I could ask, so I have to risk it on my own. Possibly I may shelter behind the dictum of that great Irish writer Oliver Goldsmith, that 'A book may be amusing with numerous errors, or it may be very dull without a single absurdity.'

My thanks are due above all to those many people who spoke so freely to me on my travels, even when they were faced with my recording machine. I must also thank Miriam Somers, who found out some facts that I needed. She belongs to the organisation Heritage Island, and I recommend anyone going to Ireland to get their Touring Guide (address: 11–13 Clarence Street, Dun Laoghaire, Co. Dublin). Otherwise, if I have made any mistakes, those who find them will enjoy the satisfaction of knowing that they know more than I do.

I definitely have to thank Jennifer Barclay of Summersdale Publishers, who sent me back my first draft peppered with shrewd and penetrating editorial comments, such as 'Why not?', 'Tell us more' and 'I don't understand'. I attended to every one of her comments as well as I could, and while it is not for me to say the book is any good, it is better than it would have been without her.

There was one point on which she would not let me have my way. I wanted to put on the cover the words 'Complete and Unexpurgated'.

'Whatever for?' she said. 'There is nothing to expurgate.'

'That is why it is complete.'

'But why say it?'

'Because,' I said, feeling rather pleased at the ingenuity of the idea, 'the grubby-minded people will buy it, hoping to find some grubby bits inside. They will be disappointed when they find there are none, but by then they will have parted with their money so it will not matter.'

Jennifer, however, seemed to think I should stick to writing and leave the marketing to them, so the cover is as you see it, the work of Peter Bailey, whose brilliant illustrations frequently brighten the pages of *The Oldie* magazine. And as there are no grubby bits, I can say, as Goldsmith said of *The Vicar of Wakefield*, 'Such as mistake ribaldry for humour will find no wit.'

To my sister and excellent friend Clarissa

FROM CORK TO GALWAY

I had a number of reasons for not taking my bicycle to Ireland until I was 64, the main one being that I had been twice before and did not like it. I went on holiday to Tipperary in 1946, and again 20 years later to Waterford on business, and it seemed to me that the countryside was dull and the people hopeless.

'Have you been in Ireland before, Mr Enfield?' they asked in 1966.

'Oh yes. After the war in 1946.'

'Ah, it would have changed a lot since then.'

'No. Not a bit. Not at all.' Fortunately they did not press the point, or I would have had to explain that all the buildings which were peeling for lack of paint in 1946 were still in the same state in 1966, and every third shop was still a pub or a bookmaker, and the walls were still supported by men who leant against them with their hands in their pockets, having nothing else to do. When I went for a third time, on the trip I am about to describe, the whole place was transformed. Nearly everyone now lived in a new white bungalow with a trim garden, and all the walls stood up by themselves.

This, they say, is due to the Common Agricultural Policy, which poured millions of subsidy into Ireland. They did not produce an extra egg, slice of bacon, or pint of milk but instead they took the money and built themselves houses.

Why, you may ask, did you want to go again? To give a rather roundabout answer to this simple question, I have found that there are three times in life when life itself improves. The first is when you leave school; the second is when your youngest child leaves home; and the third is when you leave off work. At each of these steps your freedom increases. At school you spend most of your time doing what you are told to do by other people, then as long as you have children at home you spend much of your time doing what they want you to do. When the youngest one decamps and there are just the two of you at home, you seem somehow to get a second youth. Finally when you leave off work, that is the best of all, because every day becomes Saturday.

   I had been, for many years, a local government officer, and now I was a retired local government officer, which is a good thing to be as the pension arrangements are admirable. I was, to my great delight, rich in time and comfortably off for money. I had a wife of a most tolerant nature, who remains quite calm if I propose to get on my bike and clear off for a bit. A couple of years before I had had an exhilarating time riding my bicycle across France from the Channel to the Mediterranean, and now I wanted to do something similar. The west of Ireland, they said, was very beautiful, and the whole place had come on a lot since I was last there. Possibly I had misjudged it on my earlier visits so 'To Ireland,' said I to myself, 'I shall go.'

I did not consider for a moment that I might possibly visit Ireland by any means other than by bicycle. When I got back from my bicycle trip across France people asked me, 'Which was the best part?'

'The cycling,' I replied, because it was. There is no better place from which to see a country than the back of a bicycle, and bowling along on your bike is not so much a means of getting somewhere as a pure pleasure in itself. Some of my knowing friends made what they thought were perceptive remarks about Ireland, such as 'wet!' or 'hilly!' But I brushed these aside with some resentment, as they implied I was so delicate that I must not get wet or such a wimp that I could not climb a hill.

A message reached me, via my son, from Craig Brown, that prolific humorous writer who appears in many guises, sometimes as Wallace Arnold, sometimes writing 'The Way of the World' in the *Daily Telegraph*, and sometimes in yet other forms such as a restaurant critic. He said I ought to hitch-hike in order to have interesting conversations with the people who gave me lifts, but the only effect this had was later to make me feel superior as I rode past the people who were waving their thumbs in the air.

I did, however, buy a new bicycle. The Dawes Civic which had carried me across France was now three years old, and bicycle technology had moved on in the interval, or so at least it seemed when my daughter arrived on her new Peugeot and I could not keep up with her. After a good deal of study of catalogues I decided on a Raleigh Pioneer Elite but by the time I had made up my mind it had gone out of date and become last year's model. This did nothing but good. The young man who runs the local cycle shop explained that bicycles are a matter of fashion like motorcars (or like management techniques, which have to be changed every now and then to keep management lecturers in business). Everyone wants the latest model or the latest bicycle, and as the bicycle makers cannot always think up technical advances every year they generally just change the colour or the trimmings and call it the new improved version. The fact that mine was last year's colour, a discreet dark blue, meant that it cost £250 instead of £350, as the man in the shop had bought up a batch at a discount.

He let me try it, and the real advance seemed to be in the gears. For the mountains of Ireland I thought I needed lower gears than the lowest of the six I had on the Dawes. The Raleigh had 21, an idea on which I had previously poured scorn, but now the gear change had been made so smooth that there seemed to be no loss of impetus as I hopped from sprocket to sprocket. The bicycle also seemed somehow to roll along better on the flat, as well as going up hills better, and I reckoned I was a mile-and-a-half to two miles faster than I had been before.

I changed various things from the Dawes to the Raleigh, such as my comfortable saddle, the electronic speedometer which my daughter had given me for my birthday, and the tool kit. I rode it around to get used to it, took it back to the shop to have it adjusted, and it was in a high state of readiness, and I in a high state of morale, when thieves came in the night with bolt cutters and cut through two padlocks and a steel cable and stole it. It was rather eerie going into the stable where I kept it and looking at the place where it ought to have been to find it was not there. I felt like one of those millionaires who is robbed of an Old Master and says it must have been stolen to order. There were three other bicycles but they were left behind, so the thieves had come looking for mine, knowing it was there, and I must have been under observation by unknown eyes.

Far from being disinterested, as policemen are generally reputed to be about stolen bicycles, the Sussex Constabulary treated it as the big event of the year. They sent an officer round at once who took a detailed statement, noted the frame number, carried off the severed padlocks as evidence, and did everything that could possibly be done short of recovering the bicycle. My first thought then was to go back to the Dawes, but my wife stepped in to say that she had been wondering what to give me for my sixty-fifth birthday and now she knew – another Raleigh Pioneer Elite. Back I went to the cycle shop owner who drew another from his bulk purchase stock, worked furiously on it to get it ready for touring Ireland, and I had it just long enough to decide that the standard-issue saddle was damnably uncomfortable and to change it for another by the time D-Day arrived.

As will be clear from any Irish prices that I have quoted, my trips were made before the euro had taken over from the Irish pound, or punt, since when they say the Irish have got even more prosperous. Too much so, say some, and they complain that there is an excess of house building, as in England, and even signs of people being in a hurry, which was never an Irish trait. I am sure, though, there are some things which cannot or will not change.

I found that the entire Republic was in a grand conspiracy to make sure I enjoyed myself. The whole place is one vast network of bed-and-breakfast places, so I never needed to book because wherever I was, however remote the region, sooner or later one always turned up. There is a code. The letters 'B&B', a shamrock and 'ITB approved' means the rooms will be to the high standard required by the Irish Tourist Board, and the absence of such a sign means that they may not. 'All rooms en suite' is a frequent addition to this sign. If you turn up in the afternoon they say, 'Would you like a cup of tea?' and they give you a cup of tea and a minor feast such as scones or apple pie, for which they do not charge. Under all circumstances they appear to be delighted to see you.

Furthermore, it is inexpressively beautiful. I had been prepared for this, but not for the variety. At one moment you seem to be in the Lake District; and the next you are in Cornwall; then you could be on the moon; then you are in a wilderness; and then in the most perfect valley that you have ever seen; and then beside a Norwegian fjord.

By a stroke of genius they had made it possible to cash a Eurocheque anywhere. The banks in the small towns, the grocers in the villages, and even the garages in the middle of nowhere displayed signs saying 'Bureau de Change'. When I think of the enormous security precautions in Italy, when I had to be imprisoned in a glass sentry box as a preliminary even to getting inside the bank, the cheerful way in which the Irish handed over £120 with no fuss was a restorative to one's faith in human nature. Because of all this you can be quite carefree, or at least you can in June, taking no thought for the morrow, but confident that the morrow will take thought for the things of itself. I loaded up my bicycle with much the same sort of stuff that I had taken to France except that I did not take a tent or any camping gear. This was my concession to the 'wet!' school of thought, and anyway the Irish bed-and-breakfast system had such a reputation that it seemed madness to deny myself that part of the experience. I had spent ages poring over maps and making detailed plans before I went to France, most of which was quite unnecessary, so this time I picked up a second-hand, out-of-date guidebook from a charity shop, and made a rough plan that would get me to Connemara, which seemed to be the place that was generally most admired. A good way to get to Connemara seemed to be to start from Cork, and a good place to start for Cork is from Swansea, so for Swansea, by train, I set off. As the train advances into Wales they begin writing up the names of the stations in Welsh, a language which is very well supplied with consonants but is rather short of vowels. This makes the place names impossible to pronounce and gives the impression that you are in a foreign country, but lost, as there is no means of telling where you are. Swansea, though, was given in English and I found the docks without difficulty. If things are now as they were then, everyone making the night crossing from Swansea to Cork should have a cabin if they can possibly afford it. I did not, and although it was a flat calm, several people managed to be sick as a result of getting drunk. Whether sick or not, drunks tend to be noisy, so the room with the reclining seats was not a quiet place, nor was anywhere else, and certainly not the bar. Although I had three seats to stretch out on, it was not a comfortable trip.

The ferry was called *City of Cork*, and had an Irish girl announcer but was in every other respect Polish. The captain was Polish, the notices were in Polish and the crew were all struggling with the English language with limited success. My daughter, who had crossed a month before, thought that if you said 'My baby has fallen in the sea' it would take ten minutes to find someone who understood what you were worried about.

I had expected the ferry to Cork to arrive in the city of Cork and that I would land among docks and buildings in the centre of things. Not so; I got off at a ferry terminal 12 miles away. My plan for the first day was to cycle to Macroom, which is 24 miles from Cork, or possibly to go a further 10 miles to Ballyvourney, but the ferry terminal being where it was, an extra 12 miles was inevitable. Still, it made the navigation easier as I did not have to pick my way through an urban area, but bowled along on a flat road to the outskirts of Cork, skirted round these outskirts, and pedalled in the direction of Killarney.

I was, I recall, quite cheered by my first impressions, in spite of the fact that I set off under cloud, which later became mist, and then turned to drizzle, and ended up as rain. There were green fields and stone walls and hills and it was lovely.

9

On the ferry I had noticed a young man with a shaved head and a pigtail, whose luggage consisted of a small bag and four Indian clubs such as are used by jugglers. He was hitching for lifts, and I kept passing him, and then finding him in front of me again. The third time I saw him we had some conversation, and I asked him whether the road signs in Ireland were in kilometres or miles, as I could not make it out.

'Both!' he said. 'If the sign is green it is kilometres, and if it is black, it is miles, unless it is kilometres.'

Well, I had not come all this way to find it was just like anywhere else, and I could see why places which seemed quite close on the black signs got further away on the green ones, although I was cycling towards them.

A little way out of Cork I took a minor and very picturesque road which follows the River Lee, as far as Macroom. The Lee is a little river, the road beside it is also little, and the river comes and goes, and the fields and hills are green and it was all very pleasant but I was getting wet. By Macroom I was seriously wet, as the gear which had seen me safely across France did not seem to care for a steady Irish downpour. I went and dripped all over a shop which had gone to the trouble of advertising itself in England as an antiquarian bookshop. I like that sort of shop as a general rule, and went into this one with hopes of picking up some rare work at a bargain price, but it turned out to deal only in second-hand paperbacks. Never mind, such shops are most useful to us cyclists, who like to travel light and cannot carry many books. I bought for 30p a thriller by Len Deighton, secure in the knowledge that when I finished it I could either throw it away without worrying, or graciously present it to the landlady wherever I was staying, which is what I did. I consulted the man in the shop, who recommended the Mills Inn in Ballyvourney, so, wet as I was, I went the extra ten miles. The road had been easy all the way from the ferry, I left the terminal at half past seven and reached the Mills Inn at two o'clock having done about 50 miles, very delighted with the countryside and not at all tired.

On the way I passed some thoroughbred-looking horses which were clustering under a tree, and they reminded me that there came from somewhere near here one of the best letters I have ever read. The art of letter writing is, I fear, now dead, having been killed by the e-mail, the Internet and the text message. Its death will be a great loss to English literature, but the letter I was thinking about did not come from some eminent English author but from a local landowner. It was addressed to a horse dealer with the aristocratic name of Captain Vere de Vere Hunt, who was in business in London as 'Captain de Vere Hunt's Horse Agency, under the patronage of nearly all the Royal Courts and a majority of the noble families and aristocracy of Europe'. Captain de Vere Hunt published, in 1874, a book called *England's Horses for Peace and War*, and he put at the end a collection of testimonials from satisfied customers plus this lovely letter, addressed from Castle Mary, County Cork:

> To Captain de Vere Hunt
>
> My dear Sir – I have received your letter offering me £10,000 for 'Caroline', 'Blarney' and 'Union Jack'. His Lordship's offer, through you, is liberal; but the fact is, I race and breed for my own amusement, and being easy on the score of money, I beg, with thanks, to decline.
>
> Hoping to see you at Newmarket
>
> I remain, yours truly
>
> W. Longfield.

Did ever a man conjure up in so few words and with such elegance such a picture of contentment? I often think of Mr Longfield, breeding and racing horses for his own amusement, and coolly turning down an offer of well over half a million pounds at today's rates, not because the offer was not liberal, but on the grounds that he was easy on the score of money. The phrase 'I beg, with thanks, to decline' is one that I have adopted and modified for my own use. From time to time I get out of doing something I don't want to do with the words 'I will, with thanks, decline.'

At the Mills Inn they gave me a warm welcome and an excellent room with a bath, lots of hot water and towels, tea-making equipment and television, and then, next day they gave me breakfast. And what a breakfast it was! A glass of fresh orange juice; fourteen prunes; three rashers of lean bacon; two eggs; two sausages; one tomato – all of which is known in the vernacular as a 'full fry' – plus soda bread, toast, marmalade and excellent coffee. 'If an epicure,' says Dr Johnson, 'could remove by a wish in quest of sensual gratification, wherever he had supped he would breakfast in Scotland.' This is something the Irish would dispute and certainly my Ballyvourney breakfast was high on sensual gratification.

It was served by a girl who ended every sentence with 'OK', which I found catching, so our conversation went like this:

Girl: If you want anything else, just say, OK?
E: OK.
(Pause)
Girl: Everything OK?
E: OK, thanks.
Girl: OK.

My plan for this exploratory trip was to go from Cork to Connemara and Galway, taking in the Aran Islands, and then from Galway I would go by train to Dublin, and from Dublin home. I had an admirable little guidebook called *Ireland for Everyman*, by a Mr H. A. Piehler and published in 1938. This I bought for ten pence in a book-shop run by a charity called The Lions. The Lions have it in common with Rotary and the Freemasons that they are all widespread organisations which do good works but which I have never been asked to join. I have sometimes wondered why no one ever asked me to be a Freemason, or what would have happened if I had become one, and in the same way I have occasionally wondered where Lions come from. Whoever they are, my belief is that they raise money for good causes such as buying minibuses for schools for handicapped children. One of their charitable and fund-raising activities is to run a bookshop in the village where we live. This is staffed by retired Lions who take unwanted books off the hands of some of us, and sell them on to others of us at low prices, such as ten pence.

I liked Mr Piehler and his old-fashioned style: 'The laziest and most carefree way of getting about the country is to hire a car and the services of a chauffeur'; 'One of the jolliest ways of touring in Ireland is by Motor-car and trailer-caravan'. If you don't fancy the motor-car, then says Mr Piehler, bursting suddenly into capital letters, you can get 'practically anywhere by MOTOR-BUS'. He is sound on the subject of cycling – 'one of the cheapest, Freest and most delightful ways of travelling'. He has good maps and good brief notes, and I found him invaluable.

From Ballyvourney my target that day was Killarney, and I caused a mild argument in a grocer's shop by asking whether a minor road with an incomprehensible road sign in Irish writing was the one I thought it was from the map. Everyone agreed that it was that very road, but they divided into two camps, the two women present maintaining that as a means of getting to Killarney it was impossibly 'rugged' and the one man saying that it was rugged but interesting. As a general rule, if you discuss the possibilities of going anywhere in Ireland, the people will refuse to countenance any idea except that you want to get where you are going as quickly as possible, so they always tell you to take the main road. This was the female position, and they further thought that the man was being unhelpful and obstructive in recommending the other. Nevertheless I voted for him and set off on the rugged but interesting road, and they cheerfully washed their hands of me.

In terms of being rugged it was nothing to some of the hills I had conquered in France, and I only had to get off and push for one long and one short spell. This brought me to what claimed to be the highest pub in Ireland so I went in for coffee, in the vain hope that the rain would stop while I drank it. The pub was deserted, and it took much pounding on the bell and banging about generally to raise the landlady, who put in a brief appearance to take my order for coffee, which she slammed down on the counter five minutes later and immediately vanished again. When I paid her she said it had been a pleasure to serve me, so her life must have been short of innocent amusement if she derived pleasure from the 60 seconds we were in the same room and the 20 words that we exchanged.

From there onwards the road was downhill or flat. The country was beautiful, with hills, rocks and torrents like the Lake District without the lakes. It rained in the Lake District way, more or less continuously and heavily, from about 11 o'clock, so I decided to abandon the scenic route which would have brought me into Killarney on the Kenmare road and followed the first intelligible sign pointing directly to Killarney. By no means all road signs in Ireland are intelligible to visitors. On minor roads generally, and on all roads in Connemara and Donegal, they have a tendency to be written exclusively in Irish, while the maps are exclusively in English, and this makes for difficulties. Bearing in mind that the Irish are inclined to spell a word *taoiseach* and pronounce it 'tea-shock', or spell it *dáil* and pronounce it 'doyle', and bearing in mind also that they have a different script, and further that if the signs are black the miles may be kilometres or vice versa, it is fortunate that some obliging person always turns up and asks if you are lost when you are, such as when you are standing staring at a signpost which says seven Somethings to Hieroglyphic and eight Somethings to Undecipherable.

On this occasion there was a sign saying Killarney in plain English, and I arrived back on the main road, which would have given some satisfaction to the ladies in the grocer's shop if they had known. I did not make it to Killarney that day though, because I was now convinced that what Ireland needed was a good dose of global warming. Everything that could get wet was wet, including my money, which got stained green as the dye ran from the green leather wallet inside my shorts. I was also cold, so about two miles from Killarney I decided to give up and go into the first hospitable-looking place I saw, which proved to be an isolated pub with a bed-and-breakfast sign.

I parked my bicycle and pushed open the side door and fell over a crutch. The place was packed and the man with the crutch was very sorry for tripping me up, but there really was nowhere for him to put his crutch except across the doorway. There was no sign of a landlord, so I fought my way across that room to the next one, which was equally packed, and struggled to the bar and asked if I could have a bed for the night. Yes, I certainly could, and leaving the riot to look after itself the landlord took me to an excellent room with all the conveniences of yesterday except television or kettle, and with hot radiators to dry my clothes. I had a bath which made the wetting seem almost worth it, and lulled by the hubbub from below, went to bed for a sleep. Everything was still going strong when I went downstairs at four o'clock in search of tea, so I asked the landlord if he was always as busy as this. 'Not at all,' he said, 'it is a funeral.' At a closer look I could see that the men were in crumpled blue suits. This was the second day of the funeral, which had started in another pub the day before, so by now they were all getting a bit creased. The landlord said that it used always to be the custom to carry on like this for every member of the family, but the practice was declining. This time the deceased was a particularly revered character, and so was capable of packing two large smoke-filled rooms for two days. They were all having a lovely time, and it would be a good wedding that was as jolly as this wake.

By now it was clear to me that everyone was determined that I should be enjoying myself, as indeed I was. The landlord was, if anything, a little over-anxious to please, and kept asking if everything was all right every time he saw me, and whether the room was 'to my liking'. I praised it with all the panegyric at my command, but perhaps Anglo-Saxon phlegm made me sound lukewarm, and I should have been saying 'Jesus, isn't it the most beautiful room, and wouldn't you rather be in it than eating your dinner?' or something like that. While I was having tea a small boy escaped from the wake and showed signs of plaguing me, but was quickly recaptured by his mother, who carried him off with many unnecessary apologies, and an 'Enjoy your tea, now!'

The rain was such that I could hardly have ventured out, so I had dinner where I was, with the wake going strong in the background. I had, for the first time in over 40 years, a pint of genuine Irish Guinness (having taken Jameson's whiskey in Macroom as a sort of preventative measure against the ill effects of getting wet). Guinness in Ireland, I felt sure, would be something special and have a unique quality from being brewed in Dublin (or wherever they brew it) with water from the Liffey (or wherever they get it) which would make it superior to the English version. It came, as it should, in a tall glass (I cannot abide those clumsy dimpled tankards which are generally on offer). It was, of course, a beautiful black with a delicate mist on the outside of the glass and a thin line of foam at the top, and altogether a thing of beauty. I approached it as a wine bibber would approach a fine vintage. I raised it to my nose, sniffed it with, I confess, no special result as it just smelt of Guinness. Then I brushed the foam lightly aside with my lip, took a sip and bubbled it against the roof of my mouth in a way that I learnt to copy from a wine connoisseur whom I met in Switzerland. (If you are ever asked to taste wine, I recommend you to do this bubbling business. It is quite easy and you can practise with a glass of water. I have no idea what it is supposed to achieve but it gives others the impression that when it comes to wine you know your stuff.) Then finally I swallowed my Guinness and it tasted exactly and entirely the same as all the hundreds and hundreds of pints of Guinness that I have drunk in England.

Anyone who tells you that Guinness is different in Ireland is talking rot, but it does not matter as to my mind it is universally delicious. The dinner with which it went on this occasion was pretty much the same as the breakfast I had had that morning in Macroom, a 'full fry' being what the pub was equipped to produce, and nothing else. It suited me fine. A full fry and a pint of Guinness is an excellent way to round off a hard day's cycling.

It was a short ride on to Killarney the next day. A garrulous 56 year old on the ferry had given me a glowing account of the independent hostels at which he claimed to stay in great comfort and at little cost. There was such a hostel in Killarney, so I rang the bell and was shown in by a rather surprised young man. He took me to a huge room full of bunks, like the sleeping quarters of a Gulag, from which a few villainous looking youths uncoiled themselves to see what was going on. There was a big sign at the end saying 'Beware of Thieves', and as the easiest way to beware of them was to go somewhere else, I went away in something of a hurry.

I booked into a house which had a B&B sign but not the shamrock which is the sign of ITB approval. I think the owners had hung the sign out in a speculative sort of way, and had not really expected anyone to take them seriously, so they were pretty surprised when I turned up. They gave me what looked like a child's bedroom with a frieze of teddy bears around the wall, which I think just happened to be spare at the moment. There was none of that en-suite shower business but the family and I shared the bathroom, nor can I say it was the most comfortable room of the trip, but it was much better than sleeping in a Gulag among thieves. In justice I must say that the people were extremely friendly. The husband was a keen cyclist, and directed me to a cycle repair shop where the owner replaced a vital nut at no cost, saying that I should buy him a drink if he ever came to England.

The girl in the Tourist Office gave me a route to see the lakes of Killarney. It starts at the Gap of Dunloe, which is an easy enough ride from Killarney. There you find a mass of ponies and jaunting cars, and ponies and saddles, waiting for tourists to get in or on them, to be taken up the Black Valley. The road is narrow, winds upwards and is very roughly surfaced so I was partly pushing and partly riding, and continually weaving in and out of ponies and carts. The jaunting cars were full of Germans, who are everywhere;

Americans, come to visit the homes of their ancestors; French, who cross on the ferry from Le Havre to Cork and are present in greater numbers than I have seen other than France itself; and a few Italians. One Italian was being encouraged to try yodelling at the rocks at a point where the echo is supposed to be particularly good. He could not do it as well as the driver, whose voice was louder. It is a pity that the weather is not more reliable or it would have been just the place for an open-air concert.

The scenery was spectacular, a gorge with the Purple Mountains on the left and Macgillycuddy's Reeks on the right, made more enjoyable by, of all things, sunshine. It is about a four-mile climb to the top, with a stream down the middle and with lakes appearing on either side, in one of which, according to legend, Saint Patrick drowned Ireland's last snake. All the way up there was water and rocks and irises and a white flower I could not identify but it might have been a white iris.

By the top I had overtaken nearly all the jaunting cars, so I had a free run down the other side, and found a cottage at the bottom where they gave me an excellent lunch of home-made soup and soda bread. (Soup seems to be rather a thing in Ireland, and I had it quite often for lunch, always with complete satisfaction.) There were some Germans, and later a French couple with bicycles, absolutely sitting and sunning themselves on the grass. I was

22

a bit puzzled as to how so many French people managed in Ireland, as my experience of that nation is that, however rotten one's own French may be, it is generally better than their English. They can never have encountered English as it is spoken in Ireland, not did it seem likely that Irish landladies spoke much French, so I really could not see how they succeeded in getting around or making them selves understood. In this case they got lunch by enlisting me as an interpreter, which is a counsel of despair, but it worked.

As I too sat on the grass, a pony trotted briskly past, complete with saddle and bridle but no rider. I was mounting my bicycle to see if I could catch it when the waitress appeared. 'It's one of ours,' she said, and ran after it. She caught it and put it away somewhere, and then went back to serving food, seemingly quite unconcerned that some-where among the rocks above there might be a tourist with a cracked skull who had fallen off the pony.

From that point you can get back to Killarney by putting your bicycle on a boat, and there are signs inviting you to do so. The boat crosses the Upper Lake and another time I would take it, as the ride back is undeniably rugged. This time I asked directions for the road, and for the first time encountered the word 'cross', which seems to be an omnibus term for any meeting of roads, and comprehends Y-junctions, T-junctions and cross-roads.

The waitress told me to go left at the second cross, which was actually an unsigned fork. I sensed that this was what she meant, and luckily met a man from the electricity company along the way, who told me that I had got it right.

The objective at this point is to get back to Killarney on the Kenmare-to-Killarney road, which you think would be easy from the map, but the feat is accomplished by turning your back on Killarney and pedalling vigorously in the other direction, along an unmarked but lovely road past a lot of peat-working in a valley. Eventually you make a left turn and push up and up a steep hill, which I did in a thunderstorm, the sun having gone behind black clouds an hour earlier. The storm did not last long, and eventually the Kenmare road arrived and the sun with it again. You make another left turn and it is pretty well downhill all the way from the junction, with superb views of the lakes, including the 'Lady's View'. This is so named from the ecstasies into which it threw Queen Victoria's ladies-in-waiting, and quite right too, as the Upper, Middle and Lower Lakes are all here spread out in a magnificent panorama before you.

I dodged further thunderstorms by sheltering in tunnels or teashops on the way down, and arrived dry at Muckross House, though considerably worried by the rhododendrons, which are out of control and taking over everything. Known locally as 'rosydandrums', their little seedlings are everywhere, as they love the acid peaty soil and whole mountains are covered with a blanket of boring mauve. It seems likely that the entire island will be taken over eventually. A man with a chainsaw was hacking them back at one point, but he was making very small inroads and I am sure that Nature was advancing much more rapidly than he could drive her back.

Possibly the bushes had escaped originally from Muckross House, where there is a lush and well-kept garden with lots of rosydandrums in different colours, not just mauve. Muckross House was finished in 1843, and is furnished almost entirely in straightforward Victorian style. Such is the power of fashion that it now seems both comfortable and elegant, whereas some decades ago it would have seemed funny. It was being visited by a very large party of very old American ladies, under the tender guidance of what looked like four clean-cut American college youths, whose main concern was to stop the old persons from getting too tired. They nearly caused me to lose my knapsack and anorak, which I had left at the desk at the front door as I went in. When I came back out of the back door it was almost closing time, so I hurried round to the front again, where my progress was obstructed by the octogenarian army. It would not have been polite to push and shove them out of the way, and by the time I had threaded through them in a soft and delicate manner the front door was locked. Luckily by banging and shouting for a bit I managed to get a man to come and tell me they were shut, and he gave me back my belongings.

From there to Killarney I passed by, and stopped briefly at, Muckross Abbey, which was a Franciscan friary until it was burned by Cromwell in 1652. It is very small and pretty, described by W. M. Thackeray (author of *Vanity Fair*) in 1843 as 'a little chapel with a little chancel, a little cloister, a little dormitory and in the midst of the cloister a wonderful huge yew-tree which darkens the whole place'. Then I went back to my teddy-bear bedroom and later dined on fish and chips and Guinness in a pub, where some sort of Irish jig-like songs came over a loudspeaker. I got the impression that the words, unlike those of English pop songs, might have been worth listening to, if only one could hear them properly.

Tralee was the next day's target. The road for once was fairly ordinary, but I made a deviation to Aghadoe, on the advice of my excellent 1938 guide-book.

You go to Aghadoe because from there you get a tremendous view of the Lower Lake of Killarney with mountains in the background, but the whole is now slightly spoiled by a factory which has been sited in the middle distance. A busload of Americans were walking about with labels on them saying 'Barbara' or 'David'. There were also plenty of Germans, and I began to think that for a peaceful summer holiday with lots of empty space the place to go might be Germany, which must be largely de-populated at this time of year as all the natives are busy visiting somewhere else. As well as Germans at Aghadoe, there were several French and Italians, so there was a good deal of talking in foreign tongues. It is, I may say, sometimes difficult to know in this part of the world who is a foreigner and who is not, as if there are two or more men talking earnestly together and you cannot make out a single word, it is quite likely that they are Irish and the language is English, but spoken with so thick a brogue that it could be Norwegian for all you can tell.

The sun shone all day. I ate a picnic at lunchtime in the park at Tralee, watching the cyclists ride blithely past the 'no cycling' signs. Tralee as a town is nothing much, being trippery and with music blaring out in the streets, but, as ever, all the people were very helpful, including the young policeman who escorted me to the bookshop I was looking for. Thackeray's opinion of Tralee was much the same as mine. 'As far as the country went, you pass through a sad-looking, bare, undulating country, with few trees and poor stone hedges, and poorer crops, nor have I yet taken in Ireland so dull a ride. Tralee has a handsome description in the guide-books, but if I mistake not, the English traveller will find a stay of a couple of hours in the town quite sufficient to gratify his curiosity in respect of the place.'

I spent more than a couple of hours, indeed a

whole night, Tralee being the only place where I had any difficulty in finding somewhere to stay, having to make two attempts before being taken in at a house which I reached by riding beside the ship canal which connects the town to Tralee Bay.

That evening I climbed to the top of a hill to see the sun sinking over the river estuary. On the way I passed a field of potatoes growing in couch grass, with a discreet sign saying 'Poisoned and Protected'. I suppose one way of protecting your potatoes is to make them poisonous, but it is a bit like those insects and frogs whose defence against predators is to be poisonous themselves. As they can only poison the enemy after they have been eaten, it seems to be a form of defence that only works after the enemy's attack has succeeded.

At breakfast I found a Canadian lady and her daughter who were on a one-week cycling tour. It was a package consisting of hired bicycles, accommodation, transported luggage and a guide called Kieran. There were only the two of them and Kieran on the tour, and he disappeared at night and paraded in the morning, but they did not know where he slept nor were they quite sure how the luggage got moved. There was a van which came and went, and sometimes the B&B owners drove their things to the next place in their own cars. The two of them were having a perfectly lovely time, and to travel as a pair of ladies with a Cicerone struck me as wonderfully Victorian.

They also gave me an idea for a film which I hope some Canadian film company will take up and make me rich. In my film the mother is about 42 years old and very pretty. She is by profession a lawyer in a high-powered job from which she desperately needs a break. She books this holiday, tearing herself away with great difficulty from her Toronto office, and goes with her daughter, leaving behind a husband. The daughter is about 20 years old, also very pretty, and has just finished her first year at university. As for Kieran, he too is a student, a music student who has completed two years at Trinity College Dublin, and he guides bicycle tourists as his holiday job.

So, they ride across beautiful Ireland, and they encounter picturesque Irishmen who tell amusing Irish jokes. Then one night they tell Kieran not to disappear as usual but to join them for dinner. After dinner he takes them to a bar where he is well known as he has been round the circuit several times. By demand of the crowd in the pub, Kieran gets out his flute and plays, and a man with an accordion joins in, and there is singing of Irish songs and playing of Irish tunes and there is dancing. Kieran dances with the daughter and then with the mother and then with the mother some more, and so they go on, and over the next couple of days and nights it is clear that the mother and Kieran are falling in love.

What does the daughter make of this? A mixture I think, of amusement, pleasure that her mother is having this little fling, and alarm at what will be the end of it, but they never discuss it. In one scene Kieran and the mother slip out into the darkness leaving the daughter to carry on dancing, which she does late into the night. When she makes her way back to where they are staying, as she and her mother are sharing a bedroom, she makes a great deal of banging up the stairs, calling through the door that she has forgotten something, banging down again and generally creating an opportunity for Kieran to slip out of the window if necessary. When she enters the bedroom her mother is sitting up reading a novel and we never know whether Kieran has been there or not.

It may be that the film-makers will incorporate some naked antics the way film makers like to do, but I would rather leave all that up in the air. Anyway, eventually the tour is over and they part in a *Brief Encounter* sort of way. The film draws to a close, I think, with the mother back in Toronto about to enter an important meeting when she gets an e-mail from Kieran saying that he has to see her and is coming to Canada. With tears running down her face she composes a cold, unfriendly reply to stop him coming. Then she dries her eyes and goes into the meeting. At the very end we have Kieran sitting in a corner of a

Trinity College Dublin quadrangle, with a print-out of her e-mail on the grass, playing on his flute one of the tunes to which they had danced.

There should not be a dry eye anywhere, but there is plenty of scope for Irish jokes and beautiful scenery and Irish music, and lovely tax concessions and other forms of encouragement from the Irish government, so I am confident that it will be a success from all points of view.

I devised this ingenious plot next day as I rode towards Tarbert, which is where I planned to take the ferry across the Shannon. Thinking up ideas like that is one of the things you do as you cycle along, or, at least, you do if you are alone and happen to be me. There is something about the effect of solitary cycling that has this effect on the brain. Provided there is nothing to distract you, such as a headwind or a big town, your mind is free and occupies itself with a process which can only be described as musing. I pedalled along, musing upon this and that, and then I mused upon the Canadian mother, whose cycling exploits were remarkable. She had, she told me, cycled from France to Athens taking in Delphi on the way and I think this must have been what gave me the idea of cycling in Greece myself, which I did some years later. Anyway, I mused on about her and her daughter, and about Kieran, and gradually the story took shape. I hope you enjoy the film in the, perhaps unlikely, event of it getting made.

I will also tell you, in case you take up solitary cycling on your own account, how to get over a long distance without letting it turn into a terrible slog.

I learned the secret of this from my friend Greg who used to like running in marathons, but gave it up at the age of 60.

'Isn't it very painful?' I asked knowing quite well that it is, as rowing and long-distance running are the two most painful sports that I have ever gone in for.

'The trick,' he said, 'is to set your legs going in a rhythm, then start up a train of thought on some interesting subject, and stick to it.'

This works very well on a bicycle, and what I do is make speeches. I am occasionally asked to make after-dinner speeches or give talks, so on my bicycle I go over old speeches or old talks, making them again and polishing up the same old jokes I have made before or trying to think of new ones. I tried this first in France where I had once to do 100 miles in two days in great heat. For me this is a long distance and had all the makings of a slog, but off I went, and by the time I had made an after-dinner speech twice over I had put 15 miles behind me without noticing. Then I made another such speech and I had broken the back of the first day's journey.

I did not do this on the road from Tralee, which was beautiful and serene, whereas much of the earlier road was beautiful and dramatic. The serene aspect was a pleasant change and put my mind at liberty to muse, so I mused on the Canadians. About an hour out of Tralee I stopped for a break, and was looking over a fence at the view when I was hailed with a 'What do you think?' by a man with no shirt, who was sunning himself outside his front door. I went over to explain that I had not meant to stare at his house but just to look at the hills. 'Oh,' he said, 'I thought it was the farmer come to look at his grass. Would you like a cup of tea?' So I went and sat beside him and drank tea. He was a retired bus driver who had to give up driving because of a heart attack, and was a bit sad at having nothing to do. In spite of wanting someone to talk to he did not have a lot to say, but he told me that he had a brother in Burford who runs a garage specialising in MOT repairs, and that business is brisk at the beginning and end of the month, but slack in the middle, so that was something I learnt by coming to Ireland.

A little further along I stopped to look at a shrine of the Virgin Mary, a white Virgin with a gold crown set high above the road. The postman arrived to deliver post at a cottage on the other side. The owner was old and deaf, so the conversation was conducted not *sotto* but *sopra voce*, echoing up the valley:

'HOW ARE YOU TODAY?'
'I AM WORKING IN MY GARDEN.'

'WELL, HERE IS A LETTER FOR YOU. DON'T WORK TOO HARD NOW!'

I could see the postman weaving his way from cottage to cottage on his motorbike, having little chats like that with everyone.

Later I came upon a remarkable piece of topiary. A man had written, or rather clipped 'EnRight HiLLiard' in a big bold mixture of small and capital letters on a yew hedge. This idea could easily catch on, particularly for house names and I could just see 'YoNDer ThATcH' or SHaNGri LA' springing up in suburbia. Perhaps topiary should be revived widely, and garden centres employ specialists to make and maintain such living signs among the garden gnomes.

By now I had made certain general observations about the Irish nation. In all European countries that I have visited, the word to make you halt at a crossroad is STOP and even the French use it, in spite of official resistance to the Anglicisation of the French language. It appeared to me that the Irish, while occasionally employing the word STOP, generally prefer YIELD. Yield has a rather more pugnacious sound to it, and is the sort of thing that knights in armour were given to using to each other as in 'Yield thee prisoner, Sir Knight, or by my halidome I will smite thy head off', and similar remarks. I think the martial connotation is congenial to the Irish ear, but I hope the omni-present

Germans know they are to STOP when told to YIELD.

I also observed that there was a great willingness by the Irish to be short-changed. The coinage was a bit difficult, and earlier I had given a man what I thought was £2, but was actually £1.50, for a pint of Guinness costing £1.55. 'That will do fine,' he said, and when I realised my mistake and tried to put it right, he refused to reopen the transaction. My Tralee landlady who had said she would charge me £16 gave me £5 back from my twenty-pound note and really did not want the £1 coin I proffered. In Listowel the grocer gave me two bananas for nothing and charged 20p for a 25p orange.

On the other hand, I had been in Ireland long enough to think about sending postcards home, and found that they had the most rotten cards imaginable. Either they are garish mountains or lakes with a jaunting car in the foreground, or they are twee-tourist-Irish, such as a picture of three ducks crossing the road labelled 'Traffic jam', or a donkey and a cart labelled 'The fast lane'. I hesitate to say that there is a job opportunity here in taking photographs for decent postcards, as the picture the Irish choose to paint of themselves perhaps has all the people back home doubled up with laughter, and nothing else would sell nearly as well.

★　　★　　★

I had lunch at Listowel in blazing sunshine on a bench overlooking the pitch-and-putt golf course. Two men were cutting the grass, or at least, one was riding on the tractor/mower and cutting, and the other was pointing out any little tuft of the grass that he had missed. Then they changed over. I rode on to Tarbert, where the sparkling water of the Shannon estuary came up to expectation by providing, in the words of my guidebook, 'noble views which redeem an otherwise monotonous countryside'. I am not sure about that word 'monotonous', and prefer the word 'serene' which I used earlier. At Tarbert the general friendly interest of everyone extends to include the small boys. One of them hailed me as I rode towards the ferry, with 'What's the time?'

'Five to three.'

'Ah, you are in time for the three o'clock ferry then!'

But I decided to stay the night on the side where I was, and met him again as I came back, when we had a little chat, particularly about how nice a place Tarbert is, with which he agreed. After a little, 'Where are you from?' he demanded.

'England.'

'I *thought* as much,' said he, positively hugging himself with delight at his own perspicacity.

In rural Ireland children play in the streets and talk to strangers as if there were no paedophiles, so perhaps there are none. Conceivably paedophiles

36

are reincarnated as snakes, and Saint Patrick did better than he knew when he drowned the last one.

All the way from Cork I had been seeing, and wondering about, an attractive shrub which looked as if its leaves started pink, changed to green and white, and finally became green all over, with all three stages present at the same time so you got a very varied effect from the whole. In Tarbert it was growing in a garden where a man was parking his car, so I asked him what it was. He did not know, but hurried indoors to ask his wife, who came out napkin in hand and swallowing her mouthful, to say that she did not know either. She had seen it in Cork, where it was just the latest thing, so she had broken off a twig and taken it into a garden centre and they sold her the bush. I agreed that it started in Cork and was planted all along the way to Tarbert, and walked off, thinking no more about it. In a few minutes there was a shouting and a whistling behind me, and there she was running after me as fast as her high heels would carry her, triumphantly waving the plant label which came with it. They had turned the house upside down in the interval and found it.

The plant is a variety of poplar, '*Populus Albicans*, variety *Aurora*'. It was described as a 'medium spreading tree', and the label said 'plant away from buildings', but nowhere from Cork to Tarbert was it bigger than a bush, so they must all have been

37

young, and very few were well away from buildings. I forecast that in forty years, as well as being generally mauve from the rosydandrums, Ireland will be a nation of houses with cracked foundations from poplar trees, which are noted destroyers of buildings.

Next morning I crossed the Shannon on the ferry. There was a busload of obstreperous Frenchmen shouting and showing off while we waited for the ferry, several expressing their Gallicism by publicly urinating on the quay, although there was a lavatory nearby. I think that perhaps people of any nationality, when they get into a crowd of their compatriots abroad, turn into the sort of people who ought to have stayed at home. There was also an ingenious bus, which was two-thirds seats and one-third bicycle racks. Normally I do not think I would much like to go on a coach tour, but I could be tempted by one which stayed for a reasonable time at each stop and guaranteed me the use of my bicycle wherever we were.

There is a huge power station by the ferry terminal at Tarbert, and as soon as you cross you find another on the other side, so that it looks as if the two counties of Kerry and Clare are competing to see who can generate the most electricity. On the Clare side it is at first a peaceful country ride, then at Quilty you reach the coast and suddenly seem to be in North Cornwall. There is the same grey Atlantic, the same white bungalows, the same shivering swimmers, some with surf boards and some with wet suits. There is even a Spar grocer which stocks exactly the same range, for the benefit of the same sort of campers and caravaners, as the Spar grocer in Polzeath. After Quilty comes Lehinch, which has two golf courses and is just like a Cornish tourist town such as Saint Austell, giving the impression that it wakes up for the summer and goes to sleep all winter.

I spent the night at Liscannor, where a nice lady called Kathleen gave me tea on arrival while her helpful son put my bicycle away. I had an excellent room with a shower and kettle for £15, and many apologies for the £3 single person supplement it included. The B&B at Tarbert had been full of notices, telling you to do, or not to do, this and that, such as to put your cigarette out before going to sleep, and not to dry clothes on the curtain rail or wash them in the basin. There were no such notices at Liscannor, but I asked Kathleen if she minded if I washed a shirt, and could I hang it on her line? 'Get it off your back,' she said, 'and I will take it from you!' She washed it and ironed it and put it in a thing called a hot press, and delivered it back next morning. I did no more washing on this trip as I found that all landladies responded in the same way to the same question, and I traded shamelessly on their good nature.

On Kathleen's advice I walked along to see the Cliffs of Moher, which are one of the sights of

Ireland but become invisible in a mist, which she said there might be tomorrow morning. These are indeed impressive, being about five miles of sheer rock dropping abruptly into the sea. You are directed by signs to a car park, and then you walk to the cliffs, at which point you are said to get the best view but it is swarming with people. Never mind, there is a good and clear footpath along the cliffs by which I escaped the crowds. The *Lonely Planet* guidebook says the cliffs are of 'soft shale and sandstone so unstable that few birds make their home'. My tenpenny guidebook, written by Mr Piehler, says on the contrary, there are 'layers of grit and shale, the haunt of countless sea birds'. The excellent Mr Piehler has got it right according to me, as there were plenty of seabirds wheeling and screeching above, while the sea thundered impressively below. You can see the three Aran Islands of Inishmore, Inisheer and Inishmaan spread out before you, and the guidebooks says there is a risk that you might get blown off the edge, but I didn't.

In the car park was a huge German double-decker bus with the top storey converted to bunks. It was conveying a *Jugendgruppe* of some sort, and seemed to me to provide a way of seeing the country with a minimum exposure to the people. The youths must have driven to the cliffs in the bus, got out of the bus in a body and looked at them, got back in the bus, and when it was time for bed, gone upstairs in the bus. The next stage would be to make videos of the Cliffs of Moher and other sights, and show them on the bus, which the youths need never leave at all, and the whole trip could be carried out in a car park in Hamburg.

I walked down to the village pub for supper and on the way met a lady who told me that 'with God's help' we would have a fine day tomorrow. I am all for people of a simple faith, but the theology of this puzzled me. Do any fine days arrive without God's help, and does the Almighty generally leave the weather to look after itself, and only take a hand now and again? It reminded me of the time when my mother went to buy our meat ration during the war, and remarked to the butcher, 'It is not a very nice day.'

'Madam,' he said severely, 'we must take the weather that God sends us.'

'Ah yes,' said my mother. 'But His ways are not always our ways.'

'Madam, that is very true,' he said, and gave her two extra chops above the ration.

For supper I had home-made soup, six oysters (pronounced 'ice-ters'), lots of brown bread and a pint of Guinness, all excellent, for £6.65. This sort of food was fairly easily available, but a couple of times during this trip the best I could do for dinner was sandwiches of Mothers Pride bread and plastic ham. In Tarbert the landlord had told me there were two good restaurants in the village, and I went to the one he particularly favoured, which turned out to be a café with formica tables and plastic chairs where they gave me a beefburger and tea.

At breakfast next morning (fresh grapefruit; muesli; bacon, egg, sausage, tomato, black pudding; soda bread; excellent coffee) I learned that two couples had to be turned away the night before because the house was full. I expressed my regret at the loss involved in my occupying a double room. 'Not at all,' said Kathleen. 'I never think it fair to refuse someone for being alone. It would be like turning away Our Lord!' I was a good deal overcome at this comparison, as I can say with certainty that no one had ever seen me in quite that light before.

It was good advice to visit the Cliffs of Moher on the previous evening, as in the morning they were quite obscured by mist and would have been invisible. I had thought about taking a ferry from Doolin to the island of Innisheer, and then another ferry on to Galway, but was put off by the exorbitant fare from Doolin, which was £10 one way, and £18 return, although it is only a short step across. This may not have been a very good reason, but it was the right decision, because I would have otherwise have missed the best ride of the trip so far.

The country beyond Liscannor was still extremely like Cornwall, with small fields and stone walls, though with no trees at all. The mist cleared at

Ballyvaughan and by then I was in a district called the Burren, which is rocky beyond words and the delight of naturalists because it has both Mediterranean and Arctic alpine flowers all over it. This it manages because before the Ice Age it had a Mediterranean climate and during the Ice Age it had an Arctic climate and plants from both periods now cohabit. The surface is a kind of pockmarked rock and that suits the plants very well. The pockmarks fill with water; algae form; a few grains of dust and the odd hare dropping fall in, and eventually some seed germinates there successfully. When the Burren flowers, which it does in spring, it generates a great deal of excitement among botanists because of all this floral activity. Otherwise it is generally so barren that there is little competition from the vigorous plants and grasses that might otherwise smother the more delicate items. In June, which it was for me, the outlook is of desolate grey rock, varied by patches of green in the form of short mossy grass desperately struggling for life on slabs of limestone.

But the whole arrangement makes one wonder whether one should ever throw garden seeds away. If Mediterranean seeds survive the Ice Age and are still capable of flowering you would think that ordinary lettuce seeds would come through a few years in the potting shed with no trouble at all.

After the execution of Charles I in 1649, the Irish, who had been in revolt since 1641, were comprehensively crushed by Oliver Cromwell. Edmund Ludlow, one of Cromwell's generals, arrived at the Burren from the direction of Limerick in 1652, and wrote in his memoirs, this:

> After two day's march, without anything remarkable but bad quarters, we entred (sic) into the Barony of Burren, of which it is said, that it is a country where there is not water enough to drown a man, wood enough to hang one, nor earth enough to bury him; which last is so scarce, that the inhabitants steal it from one another, and yet their cattle are very fat, for the grass growing in turfs of earth, of two or three foot square, that lie between the rocks, which are of limestone, is very sweet and nourishing.

That is a difficult sentence of 96 words, but as long as you do not panic before the end you should be able to unravel his meaning. I saw no fat cattle, nor any people, though there is evidence of them, from earlier times, in the form of an occasional dolmen or, now and then, a wedge tomb. A dolmen is officially defined as 'a tomb of vertical stone with a huge capstone'. I have not found a definition of a wedge tomb but to my eyes a dolmen looks like a big stone table and a wedge tomb like a big stone box. You have to be careful with these Irish antiquities, as we are warned by the great Irish classical scholar J. P. Mahaffy, Professor of Ancient History, and Provost of Trinity College Dublin. Writing in 1876, he tells us that 'a group of famous savants mistook a stone donkey-shed of two years' standing for a building of an extinct race of gray antiquity', and you can see why. I certainly saw a wedge tomb which would make very snug accommodation for a donkey.

From Ballyvaughan and well on towards Galway, there are rolling hills like small editions of the South Downs on the right, but all of bare rock instead of green turf. The sea appears and disappears on the left, and there are sparse fields with great outcrops of rock, and occasional rocky terraces. It was so fascinating that I could not stop, but rode all the way to Galway, having recruited my strength at a most unlikely café at Ballyvaughan, which sold, of all things, *pain au chocolat*. It was a very long ride, perhaps 50 miles, but thoroughly enjoyable until the very end, when I struggled into Galway on a busy main road in the teeth of a headwind.

I was reading that excellent book *The Aran Islands* by J. M. Synge, which I recommend most heartily to anyone travelling in these parts. Synge is one of the great Irish playwrights. His characters all come from the Irish peasantry and the dialogue is in the style that he had mastered on his visits to the Aran Islands between 1898 and 1902. He has conversation like this, with an old man called Mourteen:

'Whisper, noble person,' he began, 'do you never be thinking on the young girls? The time I was a young man, the divil a one of them could I look on without wishing to marry her.'

'Ah Mourteen,' I answered, 'it's a great wonder you'd be asking me. What at all do you think of me yourself?'

'Bedad, noble person, I'm thinking it's soon you'll be getting married. Listen to what I'm telling you: a man who is not married is no better than an old jackass. He goes into his sister's house, and into his brother's house; he eats a bit in this place and a bit in another place, but he has no home for himself; like an old jackass straying on the rocks.'

When he turns to description he gives you passages like this (a curagh being, in Synge's words 'a rude canvas canoe of a model that has served primitive races since men first went on the sea'):

Late this evening I saw a three-oared curagh with two old women in her besides the rowers, landing at the slip through a heavy roll. They were coming from Inishere, and they rowed up quickly enough till they were within a few yards of the surf-line, where they spun round and waited with the prow towards the sea, while wave after wave passed underneath them and broke on the remains of the slip. Five minutes passed; ten minutes; and still they waited with the oars just paddling in the water, and their heads turned over their shoulders.

I was beginning to think that they would have to give up and row round to the lee side of the island, when the curagh seemed suddenly to turn into a living thing. The prow was again towards the slip, leaping and hurling itself through the spray. Before it touched, the man in the bow wheeled round, two white legs came out over the prow like the flash of a sword, and before the next wave arrived he had dragged the curagh out of danger.

This sudden and united action in men without discipline shows well the education that the waves have given them. When the curagh was in safety the two old women were carried up through the surf and slippery seaweed on the backs of their sons.

The dialogue in his plays is a pure delight. Take, from *The Playboy of the Western World*, the words with which a girl called Pegeen turns down her suitor Shawn, a young farmer:

> I'm thinking you're too fine for the like of me, Shawn Keogh of Killakeen, and let you go off till you'd find a radiant lady with droves of bullocks on the plains of Meath, and herself bedizened in the diamond jewelleries of Pharoah's ma. That'd be your match, Shaneen. So God save you now!

47

My mind being filled with images of this sort taken from Synge's book, I took to photographing along the way all things relevant to the Irish way of life as he described it.

These included a boat called a hooker at the harbour in Kinvarra; some heaps of seaweed drying, presumably for fertiliser; some hay being put up into haycocks with pitchforks; and some ricks thatched with straw; – none of which could now be seen in England, unless perhaps somewhere they dry seaweed in the same way.

My plan was to spend the night in Galway and go next day to the Aran Island of Inishmore. I was standing outside the firmly-shut tourist office when accosted by an elderly man in a blue suit. Had I got anywhere to stay the night? Not yet. Well, he could tell me just the place – and he pressed a card into my hand. It was only round a couple of corners – come, he would show me. And he set off, running as hard as he could, so I mounted my bicycle and followed.

I felt immensely guilty. The sight of this rather shabby old man running for dear life while I cycled easily behind reminded me of Fanny's father in *Fanny by Gaslight*. He earned a precarious living by waiting at railway stations to see luggage loaded onto hansom cabs, and then running behind them all the way to their destination in the hope of earning a few coppers by helping to unload the trunks at the other end. He met, poor fellow, with frequent rebuffs, and his misery is most vivid. I felt as if I was taking advantage of this old man's poverty, and what could I do but stay wherever he chose to take me, in the hope that he got some commission?

It proved to be a rather dingy terrace house, unmarked by any B&B notice, not over-clean. If I look for its merits, it was central, cheap, and the loquacious landlady was devoid of any guile or harm. She showed me to my small and not very comfortable room, and gave me tea, apple pie and cream. I reflected, not by any means for the first time in my life, that an old soldier with two years' national service can sleep anywhere. Had my wife been with me I should have had to reject the house and inflict yet another rebuff on Fanny-by-Gaslight's father.

I walked about Galway that evening, and was not much impressed by the town, but I had a good meal at a pizza place which was packed and extremely noisy. Having seen Americans, Germans, Frenchmen, Italians, Canadians, Dutchmen and Danes, I had noticed that there were no Japanese in Ireland, though they are rife all over the continent of Europe. My most vivid memory of Assisi is of seeing five Franciscan monks walking past a fountain and being photographed simultaneously by 22 Japanese with cameras. The Parthenon, which always stays perfectly still and has not moved for two-and-a-half millennia, is constantly being filmed by Japanese with camcorders, as if it was their favourite grandchild winning the 100-yards in the school sports. In Ireland I had seen no Japanese, until, in Galway, two made their appearance, on the steps of my B&B.

The landlady told me that they were staying in her house, but as they spoke almost no English, she had no idea what they were doing. They had hired a car, and they went out after breakfast each day, and came back each evening, but whether they went fishing, or what they did, she was quite unable to say.

'Don't worry,' I said. 'I did not live in Japan for fifteen months without knowing how to communicate with Japanese. Leave it to me.'

The secret is to keep the conversation simple, and shout. I hasten to say, for those who do not know this, that shouting at foreigners is not unkind. I learnt this in Greece on the island of Aegina, where I stayed with a sweet old lady who used to address me in Greek with the utmost gentleness. In spite of having done half the linguaphone course, I could never understand her, but she had a very bossy daughter-in-law who used then to shout the same remarks at me, and her I always understood. From this I realised that the habit of shouting at servants in the Raj was not at all an overbearing action, it was just done to assist their comprehension.

The two Japanese appeared at breakfast next day. One wore a grey sweatshirt and looked like a shaven-headed criminal, and the other was a sort of standard-issue Japanese in a Hawaiian shirt. They spoke, as the landlady said, very little English, so I started:

'YOU ON HOLIDAY?' I shouted.

They pondered this for a while, sucking their teeth meanwhile. Finally the answer came to the surface:

'Not horriday. For writing book!'

'WRITING A BOOK! WHAT ABOUT?'

The answer was not very distinct, but to my ears it sounded as if it was 'Power houses', which I took to mean power stations. I assumed that they had given the once-over to the two competing power stations at Tarbert and Killimer, and that these would appear in some standard work in Japanese on the subject of electricity generating plants in the Republic of Ireland. Accordingly, POWER HOUSES,' I shouted. 'FOR MAKING ELECTRICITY!' and I nodded encouragingly, hoping to lead them to expatiate. They did.

'No, no! Pubbu houses. Irish pubbus.'

It emerged that they were in Ireland for three weeks, and had got a list of 100 pubs from the whiskey distillers and were working their way through them at the rate of five a day, with the aid of their hired car. Having got to this point, one of them suddenly burst into English and volunteered the words 'Not a guidebook', so I was left wondering what on earth it could be about. *One Hundred Irish Pubs* by S. Mikimoto and T. Yamamura, or whatever their names were, does not sound the most exciting of works.

The landlady had been listening with eager attention. The one thing that she had established before I took a hand was that neither of them ever took a drink, or at least not an alcoholic one. The thought of these two Japanese, with hardly any English between them, going into five pubs a day without drinking, but getting out their notebooks and scribbling instead, struck her as so extremely comic that she began to giggle. She was wearing that rather old-fashioned garment a cotton apron, and in the end she had to stuff a corner of it into her mouth and leave the room. This was lucky for me as I was in danger of catching the giggles, and had no wish to be impolite to my fellow guests. Being Japanese, I have no doubt that they had the most exquisite manners themselves, as they always have.

What could it all portend? My neighbour Ted Barclay had told me that at one time he had the agency in Japan for Waterford glass, of which he sold a lot, and for Nicholls golf clubs, of which he sold a few. His main distributor of Waterford glass was a firm called Fujita, and one day he was summoned to see Mr Fujita himself. After a little chat about glass, Mr Fujita broached what was the real purpose of the meeting, as follows:

Fujita san: You can supplying gorrufu crubs?
Barclay san: Golf clubs? Certainly. No Problem.

52

Fujita san: We are very interesting for buying gorrufu crubs.

Barclay san: You have come to the right man.

Fujita san: You can selling Irish crubs?

Barclay san: No problem! (but wondering where to get them, as Nicholls are made in Scotland).

The conversation staggered along like this for some time before Ted realised that while he was talking about sets of golf clubs, Mr Fujita was talking about golf clubs complete with clubhouses ('not crubs in bags – eighteen-hole crubs'). Perhaps I had stumbled across something similar, a market survey of Irish pubs with a view to purchase, and in due course not only would the Emerald Isle be mauve from rosydandrums, and all the house foundations cracked from poplar trees, but the pubs would be in the hands of Japanese and serving sushi.

You go to Inishmore, the largest of the Aran islands, not by boat from Galway but from Inveran, which is 23 miles along the coast of Galway Bay. There is a bus which takes bicycles, and as I waited for it I fell into conversation with an Italian family of three. I complimented the daughter on her excellent English, and she said it was like that because she lived in Wales. She had been lecturing at the University of Bangor for three years.

I was going to Inishmore because Ted Barclay's son Michael had told me not to miss the Aran

Islands, but I felt rather resentful when I found that there were three different boats, each making three crossings a day, crowded with day-trippers. Having a picture of the noble independence of the Aran Islanders as described by J. M. Synge, living in desolate circumstances and risking their lives daily in curraghs, it was disappointing to find them touting for business on the quayside, either for jaunting car rides or for bicycle hire.

Well, I was wrong and Michael was right. Most people getting off the boat turn right, so I turned left and cycled until the road ran out, and then walked among grass and rock and sea with no one around. This, I later discovered, was the walking end of the island, the other being the visiting end. I established myself in a bedroom looking out to sea and then set off for the other end. Inishmore is almost impossible to describe. It is crowded with early Christian and prehistoric remains – forts; ruined churches with unlikely names like the Church of the Four Comely Saints; holy wells; and strange pillars called dallans. There are tiny stone-walled fields which you can see have been laboriously created on slabs of limestone by men who carted sand and seaweed as described by Synge. Above all, everywhere, there is rock.

The place for which the jaunting cars set off is a fort called Dun Aengus and by the time I was making for it they were all coming back, including one with my Italian family in it. My Japanese friends came careering down a hill on bicycles, wearing baseball caps and waving merrily, clearly giving the market research a rest for the day. At the foot of the hill of Dun Aengus there was a cottage, a caravan, and a woman outside it:

'Might I leave my bicycle here, while I walk up to the fort?'

'Surely you may, but do you know anything about locks?'

'I cannot say it is one of my skills, but what is the problem?'

'Ah, there is a party of Americans coming, and all the Aran sweaters I have knitted are locked in this caravan and I think I have brought along the wrong key.'

'Let me try.' So I tried, and of course the key which would not work the lock for her would not work the lock for me, as I am not that sort of person.

'Let us try my keys,' I said.

'You have keys?'

'For my bicycle.' So I tried them and of course they did not work either.

'I could take the lock off if you like.'

'What with?'

'With a screwdriver.'

'You have a screwdriver?'

'For my bicycle.' So in the twinkling of an eye I removed the hasp and the door swung open revealing the Aran sweaters piled inside.

'Holy Mary and All the Angels,' she said, with

that blend of pious blasphemy of which only the Irish are capable. 'You've done someone a good turn today!' I could see that she felt really glad for me, and she was right, as I did feel pleased, both at helping her and at having given the quite false impression that I am a bit of a handyman.

Dun Aengus is something special. The picture postcards date it to 100 B.C. and the guidebooks call it prehistoric, and I suppose in Ireland this is the same thing. You climb the rock hill, scattered with purple flowers, and pass through three lines of jagged rocks which form the outworks, to enter the fort itself. This is vast, though not as vast as it once was, as it was originally circular and built to the cliff edge, but then part of the cliff fell into the sea. It is now a half circle with the two ends of the wall on the edge of a sheer unprotected drop of several hundred feet to the ocean. The Cliffs of Moher are nothing to it. I was only brave enough to get within a foot of the edge, and even then felt pretty frightened, especially as there seemed to be no reason why a bit more cliff should not fall away at any minute, taking me with it.

Most people were on the way back to the harbour by then and the only ones left at Dun Aengus were two American girls with sketch pads. Then they went away leaving it all to me. I lingered on for a time, savouring the air and the sounds and the utter grandeur of the sea.

I was cycling back again when a young Australian came alongside on a mountain bike.

'Did you make it?' he asked.

'I made it to the fort.'

'No!' he cried. 'To the end of the island. It's like the end of the world. Don't miss it!'

'I will have a cup of tea, and go back.'

So I rode into a pub which said it served tea, and had my first unmistakable encounter with speakers of the Irish language. The girl behind the bar was carrying on an incomprehensible conversation with three men, but she broke off to talk to me in clear, plain English, and then went back to them, and undoubtedly it was Irish they were speaking. I was in the mood to be pleased with anything, and I was pleased with that, though I sat there 'like a dog listening to music', in the words of Maurice O'Sullivan, whose book I will come to later.

Then I set off again, past the entrance to the fort and on towards the end of the island. It became rockier, more desolate, the houses further apart until there were none, not even abandoned cottages. The road got rougher, the only sound was the sea. Finally I propped my bicycle against a boulder and walked the last half mile to the very end, where there was a slipway for launching boats, but no boats. When I faced inland it was like being alone on the moon. All around there was layer upon layer of rock, in great flat slabs laid upon each other, the sea behind me, and no sign that any human being had ever set foot there before.

The next morning I found that one of my fellow guests at the B&B was a professor from Philadelphia who was over to do some research in Dublin.

'What subject?' said I.

'English.'

'They have a lot of that in Dublin?'

'Indeed they have!'

Later, as I cycled along, I perfected the conversation that I should have had with him but did not, because, as is so often the case, I did not think of it until too late. It goes like this, (and I put it in the form of a monologue, though I have no doubt that he would have joined in with expressions of admiration and astonishment, and made it into a conversation):

'Now Mr Philadelphia, I can suggest to you an idea for an article which if published in some learned periodical concerned with English Studies, would further increase your already formidable reputation. The substance of it is as follows: Take a pair of scales and on one side put the great English dramatists who wrote after the Elizabethan age, and on the other side the Irish. On the Irish scale you would put Congreve, Sheridan, Goldsmith, Wilde and Shaw, while the English side will be empty. It is a curious thing, but I cannot think of any first-rate dramatist writing in English since the end of the seventeenth century who did not come from Ireland.

Why is this so? I have no doubt at all about the correct answer, which is that the first language the Irishmen learnt was not English at all, but a kind of translated Irish. You can see this from another example from Synge's *The Aran Islands*. A young man was given an alarm clock – which is not an occasion which would normally call forth any particularly striking turn of phrase. But '"I am very fond of this clock," he said, patting it on the back; "it will ring for me any morning when I go out fishing. Bedad, there are no two cocks in the island that would be equal to it."' If something so humdrum as an alarm clock is greeted in such sparkling terms, and if everyone is talking like that all the time, then anyone of any talent at all must be bound to develop a lively imagination and a sharp ear for dialogue. If they later move to England, they write in the purest English (though perhaps, like Goldsmith, keeping a bit of brogue in their speech) and such plays as *The Way of the World*, *She Stoops to Conquer*, or *The Rivals* flow off the ends of their pens with no trouble at all.'

But unfortunately he had gone by the time I worked it out, so I had no one to say it to but myself, as I cycled back to the ferry.

From Inveran, having crossed back to the mainland, I rode straight up to a place called Maam. I had to have a few lessons in how to pronounce it, but in the end I realised that you should say it as if you were a sheep, 'Maa-m', like that. On the way back to Maam it was all stone walls and stony fields, but then you come into a river valley with big fields, good grass and the Maamturk mountains above. It is called 'Joyce's Country'. I have crossed Canada and France from side to side, lived in Germany, Thailand, Hong Kong and Japan, visited Italy four times and Greece more often that that, but I have never been in a more beautiful place than Joyce's Country. The sun shone, and the combination of hills and rocks and water and greenery was perfect.

Having found it, I could not leave it, so I took a room for two nights. I went to the door of a promising-looking house with an ITB sign and a flourishing garden, I rang the bell and a lady with red hair opened the door, gave me a big smile and said. 'How are you?' This kind enquiry after my health by a complete stranger took me by surprise at first, and I wondered sometimes what would happen if I said, 'I've got a bit of a headache' or 'I think I might have a cold coming on'. Anyway, I hadn't, so I didn't, and of course 'How are you?' is no different in meaning from 'How do you do?' and does not lead to a discussion of one's medical condition. The best answer, I decided was a hearty 'hello!' and then get down to the business of a room. On this occasion I dropped my usual hint about washing and this very friendly lady carried off my shorts, vest and pants to wash them, 'rather than having you slubbering about upstairs'.

★   ★   ★

The next day I had a leisurely ride to Leenane, along an utterly beautiful valley. Around Maam there are no walls but big green fields with good grass, and there were sheep and cows wandering over the road and, once, a pony. It made a sudden change from Galway, where the country was all stone walls and stony fields.

At Leenane you are at the head of a long inlet from the sea, which the guidebook calls a fjord. Having never been to Norway I must take their word for it, but if Norway is like this it is wonderful. Along the way I met an old lady who was washing clothes in a stream. She said she was happy about everything in Joyce's Country except the midges and the rain, and as neither was in evidence at the time, the whole place seemed to me to be without a fault. She also said that she drew water for her house from a well; that she always got up early to feed the lambs and to avoid the midges; and that while I was here I should visit the Aasleagh Falls (pronounced Ashleigh), so I did, and they are very fine.

The river here is, I believe, the Erris, though there is nothing on the spot to tell you so. It makes, at Aasleigh, a kind of miniature Niagara which to my mind is a proper sort of waterfall. There are some waterfalls which are no more than long, thin airborne streams of water, but I much prefer those which come about when a reasonably broad river arrives at a precipice and tumbles over the edge. The Erris was doing exactly this, the width being,

I guess, about 40 feet and the fall into the pool below about the same, the whole scene embellished with a plentiful growth of rosydandrums, and the sun glistening in the falling water.

On the way back I got a puncture, so I went into a house to ask for a bucket of water. An old lady opened the door, and asked me how I was, but added immediately that everyone was out except herself and her four-year-old grandson, and that neither of them was empowered to take decisions about anything. Perhaps she thought I was a carpet salesman, but when I explained what I needed she gave me a bowl of water, and her grandson came along to help. Grandmother kept putting her head out of the door to shout 'Don't be a nuisance to the man, now', but I assured her that he was actually helping the man, which he was, because once I got the inner tube out in the open I got him to put his thumbs on each side of the hole so that I did not lose the place while fumbling for the glue and the patch. When it was done she shouted at him to fetch the man some clean water to wash his hands, and to fetch the man some soap, and to fetch the man a towel, so the man got pretty good service altogether.

The next day I set off back towards Galway, passing the north end of Lough Corrib. It was in these parts that the word 'boycott' was added to the English language, and to understand the episode of Captain Boycott one needs to take a quick view of some aspects of Irish history.

For centuries Ireland was regarded by England as a colony to be exploited by all possible means. By degrees and at different times the Irish were deprived of nearly all their land. Then, in the early eighteenth century, as a means of supposedly promoting their loyalty to Protestant England, every effort was made to deprive them of their religion as well. The two go together, but I will at this point deal mainly with the land.

There were numerous confiscations of land in the reigns of Elizabeth I and James I. 'Still more under Cromwell,' says the English agriculturist Arthur Young, who spent three years in Ireland from 1777 to 1779. Cromwell, he says in his *Tour in Ireland*, 'parcelled out an immense proportion of the kingdom to the officers of his army, the ancestors of great numbers of the present possessors: the colonels of his regiments left estates which are now eight and ten thousand a year, and I know several gentlemen of two and three thousand pounds a year at present which they inherited from captains in the same service. The last forfeitures were incurred in that war which stripped and banished James II. Upon the whole nineteen twentieths of the great kingdom changed hands from catholic to protestant. The lineal descendants of great families, once possessed of vast property, are now be found all over the kingdom in the lowest situation, working as cottars for the great

great grandsons of men, many of whom were of no greater account in England than these poor labourers are at present on that property which was once their own.'

Much of the land was in the hands of absentee landlords, living away from their estates, mainly in England. Arthur Young lists 194 absentees, including such eminent names as the Duke of Devonshire with 18,000 acres, down to Edmund Burke with 500. There are, he says, 'absentees who expend large sums on their estates in Ireland', but as a general rule 'The landlord at such a great distance is out of the way of all complaints, or which is the same thing of examining into, or remedying evils; miseries of which he can see nothing, and probably hear as little of, can make no impression. All that is required of the agent is to be punctual in his remittances, and as to the people who pay him, they are too often, welcome to go to the devil, provided their rents could be paid from his territories. This is the general picture.'

The income from these estates was collected either by agents or by 'middlemen'. These middlemen were themselves principal tenants, who sublet parcels of land to small farmers often at exorbitant 'rackrents'. 'Living upon the spot,' says Arthur Young, 'surrounded by their little undertenants, they prove the most oppressive species of tyrant that ever lent assistance to the destruction of a country. They relet the land, at short tenures, to the occupiers of small farms; and often give no leases at all. Not satisfied with screwing up the rent to the uttermost farthing, they are rapacious and relentless in the collection of it.'

Any tenant who could not pay his rent was evicted.

No traveller to Ireland could fail to comment on the rural poverty which he found. William Cobbett, a radical politician and champion of the poor, though used to the sight of poverty in England, was deeply shocked by what he found in Ireland as late as 1834.

> I went to a sort of hamlet near to the town of Middleton. It contained about 40 or 50 hovels. I went into several of them, and took down the names of the occupiers. They all consisted of mud-walls, with a covering of rafters and straw. I took particular account of the first that I went into. It was 21 feet long and 9 feet wide. The floor, the bare ground. No fire-place, no chimney, the fire (made of potato-haulm) made on one side against the wall, and the smoke going out of a hole in the roof. No table, no chair: I sat to write upon a block of wood. Some stones for seats. No goods but a pot, and a shallow tub, for the pig and family both to eat out of. There was one window, 9 inches by 5, and the glass broken half out. There was a mud-wall about 4 feet high to separate off the end

of the shed for the family to sleep, lest the hog should kill and eat the little children when the father and mother were both out, and when the hog was shut in; and it happened some time ago that a poor mother, being ill on the straw, unable to move, and having her baby dead beside her, had its head eaten off by a hog before her own eyes! No bed: no mattress; some large flat stones laid on other stones, to keep the bodies from the damp ground; some dirty straw and a bundle of rags were all the bedding. The man's name was Owen Gumbleton. Five small children; the mother, about thirty, naturally handsome, but worn into half-ugliness by hunger and filth; she had no shoes or stockings, no shift, a mere rag over her body and down to her knees. The man BUILT THIS PLACE HIMSELF, and yet he has to pay a pound a year for it with perhaps a rod of ground! Others, 25s. a year. All built their own hovels, and yet have to pay this rent.

To get back to Captain Boycott, the harvest of 1879 was one of the worst on record, and tenants in many parts of Ireland were unable to pay their rents. An organisation called the Land League was formed to campaign for reduced rents and fair treatment for tenant farmers, having as its President the great Irish patriot Charles Stewart

Parnell. One of the league's tactics was that, when any tenant was evicted, no one should apply to take on the vacant farm, and to enforce this rule, Parnell, addressing a meeting of farmers said that 'when a man takes a farm from which another has been evicted you must shun him on the road-side when you meet him, you must shun him in the streets of town, you must shun him at the shop counter, you must shun him in the fair and in the market-place, and even in the place of worship.'

Captain Boycott was far from being such an impoverished tenant. He lived in some style at Lough Mask House, a few miles north of Lough Corrib, from where he acted as agent to the Earl of Erne. He had refused the lower rents offered by distressed tenants and set about issuing 'processes of eject-ment' on those who would not, or could not, pay the full amount that he demanded. E. A. D'Alton, in his *History of Ireland* of 1910, gives this account of what happened next:

> The tenants retaliated by attacking the process-server and driving him into the shelter of Lough Mask House. But further, partly by persuasion, principally by terror and threats, they got Captain Boycott's servants and labourers to leave him. No one would save his crops, no one would drive his car, the smith would not shoe his horses,

the laundress would not wash for him, the grocer would not supply him with goods; even the post-boy was warned not to deliver his letters. The Ulster Orangemen came to the rescue, and fifty of them, escorted by police and military with two field-pieces, came to Lough Mask. They saved the Captain's crops, valued at £350, but at an estimated cost to the State and to the Orange society of £3500; and when they left Lough Mask House became vacant, for Captain Boycott fled to England. The genial and witty parish priest of the Lough Mask district, Father John O'Malley, suggested to his friend Mr Redpath, an American journalist, perplexed for a suitable word, that boycott was a better word than ostracise, the latter being too difficult to be understood by the people. The hint was taken, the word used in the sense gradually gained currency and became incorporated in the English language, and of all the weapons used by the Land League none was more dreaded by landlords and their friends than the terrible weapon of boycotting.

So much for Captain Boycott. Leaving Maam and heading for Galway I came to the town of Cong at the north end of Lough Corrib. They made a film called *The Quiet Man* at Cong and this has obviously supported the town ever since, as it is full of signs directing you to the places where filming took place, and pilgrims came from all over the world to see it. When I arrived Cong was plastered with posters and in a state of excitement as voting was about to take place in a referendum on the Treaty of Maastricht. Those opposed to the Treaty had devised the ingenious slogan of 'Don't be Maas-tricked' and this was much in evidence. However Mr Jacques Delors, who was at that time at the head of the European Union, had come up with an offer of a judicious bribe in the form of six billion pounds to be doled out at the rate of one billion pounds a year for six years and this worked, or perhaps I should say it did the Maas-trick, as Ireland voted 'Yes'.

From Cong I set off to ride down the east side of Lough Corrib, which is some 20 miles long and one of the biggest Irish lakes. Some say that it has 365 islands, one for each day of the year, but others say that this claim is made for several lakes in Ireland and that the figure is always just invented for the benefit of tourists. I got a lecture about Lough Corrib from a postman when I stopped to ask him for directions. He wished me to know how beautiful it was and how I was about to take the best photographs of the trip, as there was no finer sight in Ireland than the islands of Lough Corrib. It was very fine, and it was a delightful ride, with the lake on my right all dotted with islands, and a superb display of fuchsias flowering all along on my left. The postman, though, had over-estimated me as a photographer. My snap of three fields with a stretch of water and a few islands beyond by no means did the lake justice.

I stopped that night midway between Cong and Galway and asked my landlady that night (who had given me a lovely room overlooking the lake) if she could lend me something to read. This caused embarrassment, as reading was not much in her line, but she asked her daughter, who was just as embarrassed, as she only read romances. I fancy she did not want me to know what they were like, but in the end they asked if I had heard of Gay Byrne.

'Isn't he the man who got the Northern Ireland Secretary to sing "Clementine" on television?'

He was indeed. Gay Byrne was a household name in Ireland, where he had a hugely popular television chat show. I only know of him because Peter Brooke, who was at that time the Secretary for Northern Ireland, came on his show and was somehow persuaded, as part of the interview, to sing the opening verses of 'My Darling Clementine'. Why or how he was persuaded to do this, I do not remember, but he was, and it was a mistake. I have a clear picture in my head of Peter Brooke as a usually dignified and slightly ponderous character, the sort of man who gets to be Chairman of the Conservative Party, which was his previous job. Although he had a perfectly reasonable singing voice his rendition of 'Clementine' was, to be frank, undignified and tending towards the ridiculous. For which reason, of course, English television seized on it and showed it on the news in England, and so I knew about it.

Having established that I was aware of Gay Byrne, my landlady lent me his autobiography which, greatly to my surprise, was interesting. It was interesting about his early life, when his father was a lighterman taking barrels of Guinness up and down the Liffey, and even more interesting about his later life, when he entrusted all his money to the most respected accountant in Dublin, who stole it all and died, leaving him with no cash but big debts to the tax collector. I thought there was a lesson here for my comedian son Harry, and I had better hurry home and tell him.

This trip, as I have said before, was to be an exploratory venture to see whether I had done Ireland an injustice in my earlier melancholy assessment of its merits. Well, I had. Everything about the country had delighted me. Ireland and Greece vie in my estimation as to which is the most beautiful, and I cannot possibly settle the point, as whichever one I am in at the time seems to be the winner.

Ireland was full of kind and hospitable people, and as for cycling, it seemed a sort of paradise. The roads were very far from busy, and the drivers all scrupulously careful not to run me over. They appeared to feel that an elderly man on a bicycle deserved some sort of recognition, which from women often took the form of a wave, but, in the case of men, a more subtle gesture. It took me a while to recognise this, but after a day or two I noticed that when a car or lorry was coming towards me, as we got close the male driver would give me a nod, and without letting go of the steering wheel, would raise his right forefinger and point it to the sky. You might think that would not be very notice-able, but Irishmen tend to have large hands with large forefingers, and if you are alert to the gesture it is plain enough. Once I had realised what it was, whenever a vehicle approached I always fixed my eyes on the driver's hand, and when the forefinger went up I acknowledged it with a wave. This mutual exchange of courtesies contributed to the general bonhomie and abundance of feel-good-factor which cycling in Ireland managed to bring on.

I felt that I could have cycled on and on, but my plan had been to go from Cork to Galway and back from Dublin, for which I had set aside a fortnight, and time was nearly up. So next morning I rode into Galway and took a slow, uncomfortable train to Dublin, having with some difficulty persuaded the booking clerk that my European Senior Travel Card entitled me to a discount on the fare. And Dublin, I regret to say, was a disappointment.

I am ready to believe that this was my fault, but Dublin and I did not hit it off. I booked into a scruffy, cheap hotel in what seemed at the time to be a scruffy run-down city. At the hotel I asked some questions of a fellow guest, and I got such a hostile answer that I concluded he must be in the IRA. I walked along O'Connell Street which Mr Piehler's guide said was 'one of the finest and widest thoroughfares in Europe'. Wide it may be, but fine it was not particularly, or not more than Oxford Street in London, and it seemed to have no more to offer than a collection of shops and banks, and a department store about as interesting as Selfridges, of which it is, I believe, a smaller replica. I went to Trinity College, which is indeed a most handsome edifice, but even Trinity was against me as they had locked away the *Book of Kells*. This, as you may well know, is one of the world's most beautiful books, being a wonderfully illuminated manuscript of the gospels, made at the monastery of Kells in the eighth or ninth century. It is generally on display and of course I wanted to see it, and it added to my general disgruntlement that I was not allowed to do so.

In my unfavourable view of Dublin I was entirely wrong, and I revised it altogether on my later trip. The next day, though, I was glad enough to shake the dust of Dublin from my feet, ride to the docks and cross to Holyhead. The only excitement of the journey home lay in riding from King's Cross to Victoria via Trafalgar Square, Whitehall and Victoria Street. To those who cycle about London all the time this will not seem exciting in the least, but you must remember that I came fresh from

73

the empty roads and peaceful scenes of western Ireland and to take on the London traffic in this way was, I felt, rather a dashing, enterprising sort of thing to do. I got home to find in the succeeding weeks that I had become a bit of an Iro-bore, because I insisted on telling everybody what a magnificent place Ireland was and how they ought to go there on their bicycles. I had not finished though. There was a lot of the west coast still to explore, which I would do two years later.

INTERLUDE – SOME PRELIMINARY ENCOUNTERS WITH THE IRISH

I made my first visit to Ireland when I was 17, to stay with some friends who had emigrated from Sussex because the fox hunting was too slow, and they wanted to risk their necks by galloping over the stone walls of Tipperary.

Apart from the dreary countryside and its general air of depression, my main memory of Ireland in 1946 is of my hosts' car with a broken spring. They had broken it by driving too fast over the terrible roads, and the ride in the back seat was even more violent than it would have been otherwise. On one occasion we gave a lift in the back to a farmer, and the driver said, by way of apology, 'I'm afraid we have a broken spring.'

'We have,' came the enthusiastic answer. 'It is. 'Tis terrible weather. Terrible!'

Admittedly the month was April, but this made me realise that in Ireland you can link unreasonable nouns with impossible adjectives and apparently make sense. You could, I am sure, point towards the evening sky and say 'That is a gracious sun.' You would then get an answer such as 'A man could burn his eyes out looking at it' or 'You would hardly know it was there from the sight of it', depending on circumstances; and the conversation would be regarded as perfectly satisfactory.

The broken spring also affected the Guinness which we sometimes carried. Guinness in those days came in bottles with corks in the top, and every now and then there would be a popping noise as a cork flew out and Guinness foamed all over the back seat.

In between my visits of 1946 and 1966 I spent two years doing my national service, in an Irish regiment, the 8th King's Royal Irish Hussars. They were stationed in Germany, and are now defunct, having been merged and re-merged with other regiments. The number of Irishmen in the army varies from time to time. At one period in the nineteenth century rates of pay and general conditions were so bad that hardly anyone but starving Irishmen would enlist, and the Welsh Fusiliers were Irish to a man (and perhaps to a goat as well, as they have a regimental goat.) This was no longer so, and as Englishmen had to do national service while Irishmen did not, there were not all that many Irishmen in the 8th Hussars. They kept up the regimental Irishness by wearing hats embroidered with shamrocks and calling their squadrons 'R', 'B' and 'C' squadrons. 'R' squadron was spelt 'A' squadron but they pronounced it 'R' as Irishmen were supposed to be unable to say 'A' and always said 'R', or 'Ah' as you prefer.

They also had a lot of horses, housed in a magnificent stable block built for the German Panzer regiment whose barracks in Lüneburg had been taken over by the British. Keeping horses is an Irish tradition, but in this case it was mainly to do with being a cavalry regiment, and they had no more horses than their predecessors in Lüneburg, the Royal Scots Greys. The 8th Hussars, when posted to Germany to relieve the Greys, took over from them the barracks, the tanks and the horses. The tanks were found to be in very bad condition, and it was explained that 'the Greys do not like starting the tanks, as it frightens the horses'. (I have written that in ordinary English. From the mouth of a proper cavalry officer it would come out as 'Ve Gweys don't like startin' ve tanks as it fwitens ve horses.')

The horses were kept purely for pleasure and not for any military or ceremonial purposes. They were looked after by a mixture of German grooms who were on the payroll as clerks and storemen, and 8th Hussars troopers. There are those who argue for the return of national service on account of the moral benefit it conveyed, which, for those who spent two years of service to Queen and Country in mucking out the horses ridden by the officers of the 8th Hussars, may not have been very great.

I was a second lieutenant, although they called us 'cornets', like ice-cream cones, because they liked to cling to the obsolete title of 'Cornet of Horse'. This, says the *Oxford Dictionary*, was the rank of 'the fifth commissioned officer in a troop of cavalry. (Not now in use)'. It was in use in the 8th Hussars all right, and my letters came addressed to 22711717 Cornet Enfield, though I was not the fifth commissioned officer in a troop, but the only one. When I arrived they put a whole troop of three tanks under my command, until they realised what an inefficient officer I was, most particularly because I couldn't read a map and so my troop and I kept getting lost. Then they took me off my duties as a troop leader and made me Assistant Adjutant, an office job where they thought I would do less harm.

We had a German riding master, a Prussian Count who had lost his estates in East Germany and was on the strength as a clerk. He was an excellent horseman, and we used to ride before breakfast and after tea, under his instruction. One day they went to the army remount depot and came back with a new chestnut horse called Jester. Different people rode him around, and he proved to be very sensible, so he was entered, along with several others, in a hunter trial run by the 7th Hussars, and I, having no horse of my own, was put down to ride him.

(In a hunter trial you canter for a couple of miles, jumping over obstacles as you go, or at least that is the idea. It was something I knew about but had never gone in for myself – and neither, as I was to discover, had Jester.)

Two days before the event, we were ordered to the riding school for some jumping practice. I have said that Jester was sensible, and he certainly had his feet on the ground, nor had he any intention of taking them off it, or not all four of them at once. No one had discovered that he had never jumped anything in his life, and did not mean to start now. Any pole that he could not step over he either demolished with a sliding tackle, or else turned his back on it, and the second-in-command of the regiment standing behind him with a big whip exercised no influence at all.

But there was no retreat. Two days later Jester got into a horse box and I got into somebody's car, and off we went. Although the first event was for individuals, not for teams, they started us in three's, but we did not have to keep together. My three approached the first thick brush fence in line abreast, with me in the middle. The horse on either side jumped over the top, while Jester went straight through the middle like a cannon ball, punching a big hole and emerging on his knees, with me up near his ears. When he got up, he found his friends had gone on without him, so he set off to join them, destroying every obstacle in his path.

There were not many jumps still standing after Jester had passed by. We had smashed and splintered our way round the first half of the course, when Jester, who was no fool, decided there must be an easier way of doing this, and took to climbing over the top instead of barging through the middle. This method of getting along is, among other things, slower than jumping, so we reached the finish to huge ironic cheers with about 144 penalty points, 200 time faults, and they announced a twenty-minute break while they rebuilt the course.

We were also entered in a team event, and this time the three of us did have to keep together. I think Jester must have had a word with the others in the interval because he began jumping over things, and any damage he did was mainly due to inexperience. The sixth fence was a drop hedge. This means that the landing side is lower than the take-off, which is something that can cause difficulty to horse and rider alike. Jester, having no idea what was involved, flew over it like a swallow and landed like a cat, and as I cantered on in astonishment, I realised that I was alone. The other two were on the ground, as one horse had come down, and the other rider had fallen off. I trotted back and from the commanding heights of Jester's back, enquired in my most condescending manner 'Are you all right?' They were, but one of them was a major, and as the senior officer present he decided we should retire, as his horse was out of control.

This was fine by me, but then I found out that while Jester and I had been vandalising the novice course, one of the horses in the team for the open event had gone lame, so they had either to find a substitute, or scratch the team. The final fence on the open course, right by the finish, was also a drop hedge. They had made it far too big, it was slippery on the take-off side, there was a bog on the landing side, and horse after horse was falling over. I stood beside the Colonel of the 8th Hussars, my natural enjoyment of the spectacle of senior officers rolling in the mud utterly dispelled by terror, as he debated where or not to honour Jester and me with promotion to the first team. Finally he decided against it, not from any fear of rendering me paraplegic, but because he thought it might be hard on Jester. 'He is a bit green, Colonel,' I said, trying to sound nonchalant, though he was not half as green as I was round the gills, at the thought of riding him over that precipice.

And so they scratched the team, and I lived to tell the tale. Jester must have been dead for many years, but if I could find his grave, in consideration of the amusement he gave to other people that day, I would put up a headstone with the words: 'Jester – by name and by nature'.

The colonel was an amusing man, a fine soldier, and always encouraging to me. I mean no disrespect when I say that I also remember him as being short of breath and talking like a character called Jogglebury Crowdey in the novels of the nineteenth century sporting novelist R. S. Surtees. I was present as Assistant Adjutant when he disciplined a trooper (who I will call Fulleylove) for punching a sergeant (who I will call Hooley) on the nose at an Other Ranks Dance. Fulleylove's problem was that he wanted to marry a German girl, and the colonel would not let him, on the grounds that no decent German girl would go out with a British soldier and he was not having any of his men marrying tarts. In punching Sergeant Hooley, Fulleylove was actually trying to punch his way out of the army with a dishonourable discharge, so that he could get on with marrying his girl. Sergeant Hooley, who was indeed Irish, gave his evidence:

'Sorr. On the day and date stated, sorr, I observed the accused creating a disturbance, sorr. I approached him and remonstrated with him, sorr. Five minutes later I observed the same occurrence occurring again, and I approached the accused and he struck me. Sorr!'

'Well Fulleylove,' said the colonel, 'what have you got to say?'

'Nothing to say sir,' said Fulleylove gloomily.

'Well Fulleylove,' said the colonel, 'you are a swine (gasp). You are a swine (wheeze). Sergeant Hooley and I were your guests (gasp) and we don't go to parties (puff) to be hit by our hosts. (Wheeze). Twenty-eight days. March out!' And so, to much shouting by the Regimental Sergeant Major, Fulleylove marched out to spend 28 days in the guardroom.

The sentence was not severe, but I rather doubt

if the Colonel's remark about hosts not hitting their guests really registered with Fulleylove, or was likely to influence his future conduct, as it was not any lack of manners that led him to thump Sergeant Hooley. He had been a most promising soldier, rose to the rank of corporal and was bound to make sergeant before long, until love struck. Then he started on his campaign of deliberate revolt against the army which so far had got him 'busted', as it was called, down to trooper, which is the cavalry equivalent of a private soldier. Everyone thought this was very sad, but no one could think of anything to do about it – not that they gave it very much thought at all, being busy with other matters.

One of my better military memories is of being in the adjutant's office when they came round to make an inventory. To make an inventory in the army a sergeant marches in front and a corporal marches behind, holding a clip-board; the sergeant shouts out a description of each item in the room and the corporal writes it down. Every item had its own special definition, such as that table which was found in every barrack room and known as a 'table, soldiers', six foot.' In the adjutant's office there was a single coffee table which to me was no more than a small coffee table, and an auctioneer would have catalogued it as such, but it went into the inventory under its full military description of 'tables, nest of three, two deficient.'

*   *   *

The most thoroughly Irish officer was Richard Dill, now unfortunately deceased. He was the ideal cavalry officer, being very good-looking, witty, rich and a superb horseman, with an estate in Limerick. He went in for romantic things like winning the Grand Military Gold Cup on a horse that he had bred himself, and getting himself left a lot of money but with a proviso in the will that he must change his name to Murray. This caused him some anxiety, as he wanted the money but not the name. First he changed his name, and it was given out in regimental orders that Major R. P. G. Dill would henceforth be known as Major R. P. G. Murray. Then he started legal proceedings to have that part of the will set aside, and kept disappearing to England for consultation with lawyers. In the middle of it all, on a day when he was due to ride in a steeplechase, he said to me, 'I say Eddie, I hope I don't break my neck. I don't want to go to my grave a *Murray*!' I came across him years later in a footnote to a legal textbook (Murray and Barclays Bank vs Dill) from which I learned that he had triumphed in the courts and gone back to being Dill.

When I was demobbed, I went to work in Hong Kong, which is where I met my wife, who is English by upbringing but Irish by ancestry. The English side of her is definitely uppermost and she approaches the Irish with a good deal of wary reserve.

In a nutshell she thinks they are not only unreliable in almost every way, but also, according to themselves, all their sins and peccadilloes are to be forgiven because they are charming, and because, being Irish, they cannot be expected to behave like other people. This is, in a way, similar to those people who think they are entitled to be terribly rude on the grounds that they come from Yorkshire. 'I'm a Yorkshireman and I speak me mind,' they say, as a prelude to some offensive remark. Irishness is more subtle. To give you an example of the sort of Irish behaviour which greatly irritates my wife, I will tell you that we once asked a man called Gorman to dinner and he arrived an hour and a half late, keeping the other guests and ourselves waiting. In such circumstances any normal person, such as me, would arrive with profuse apologies, proffering excuses and possibly chocolates or flowers to the hostess. Not so Gorman. He simply burst through the door in a boisterous manner, exclaiming as he came 'If this was a quiz could you guess which was the Irishman of the party?' I really believe that he thought that unpunctuality was part of his Irish charm, an idea which may well be widespread. I have not had much experience of Irish railways, but if they are anything like ours, then the fact that the trains might not run on time is very likely to be regarded as one of the delights of the country, instead of being an aggravation as it is over here.

The reason why my wife is Irish is that her parents were, though when I knew them they were established in England. They were Catholics originally from Cork, with the unlikely names of Jenkins and Bennett (Bennett being my mother-in-law's maiden name). You would think that people called Jenkins and Bennett would be Protestants planted in Ulster by Cromwell to oppress the native population, but they were definitely of the other sort. My mother-in-law was very keen on clothes and fashion but she did not have much money. She dealt with this by hunting for bargains at sales, an activity which she raised to the level of an Olympic sport. By 'sales' I mean things like the Harrods sale, which in those days was a real sale and not the poor thing it is now. Before Harrods was spoiled by the Egyptians they never bought anything in, they just reduced the prices of the stock in hand. If things did not sell at the reduced prices they reduced them again, and if they still did not sell they reduced them yet again. On the last day of the sale, in order to shift the stuff that was left they brought the prices down dramatically, and that was my mother-in-law's big moment.

All year round she would prowl through Harrods like a hungry tigress marking down the likely items which seemed to be sticking in the shop and were therefore candidates for the sale. She called this process 'watching'. On the first day of the sale she would be there, doing a bit more watching, but never buying. As the sale progressed and prices came down but goods disappeared, she would become more and more excited and nervous, wondering whether to move in on the coveted items, or to risk waiting for a further reduction. I have said it was like a sport, and it was not exactly a blood sport, thought knowing the speed with which she moved through the crowds armed with an umbrella I expect there were some casualties. It had, however, a certain similarity to fox hunting, in which it is not uncommon for the huntsman to throw the reins of his horse to someone else to hold, while he plunges among the hounds to perform the last rites on the fox. In the same way my mother-in-law would fling my wife, then a babe in arms, to a shop assistant with instructions to hold her while she moved in for the kill, or as she herself put it, while she 'pounced'.

I have to say that this tireless pursuit of bargains meant that she was always strikingly and elegantly dressed. She had a certain vanity about her appearance, and always considered that any picture of herself was spoilt if my wife, as a child, got into it. She used to then cut her out with scissors and throw her away, and my wife has a number of photographs of her mother which have holes in them for this reason.

My father-in-law was perhaps a less colourful character. In his later years he bought all the newspapers every morning and spent much of the day sucking his pipe and doing the crosswords. Occasionally something would strike him as funny in the text of the paper, and he would demand silence and read it out loud. In his thick Irish brogue he would say: 'Here's a good one. Listen to this.' Then he would look round the room over the top of his newspaper to see that we were all attending, and read out the bit that had tickled his fancy, before going off into a series of gasping, wheezing chuckles which were, in Sam Weller's phrase, 'a good deal in the appleplexy line', and left him struggling for breath and exclaiming 'Oh dear, Oh dear, Oh dear.' He smoked continually, never took exercise or ate vegetables, and lived to be 83.

Naturally my parents-in-law told me that Ireland was a magnificent country, while my wife was telling me that it was not, though her first-hand experience of the country was limited to no more than a few weeks as a child. Even these, I may say, she seemed to have enjoyed, as they left her with happy memories of paddling in the sea off County Wicklow and getting lifts in pony traps, but she still took this pessimistic view of the Irish character. On the other hand, my neighbour Ted Barclay, who had worked in Ireland for several years, kept insisting that there was no place like it on Earth, and that it was the only place to which he ever wanted to go on holiday, and that any sensible person who could live there would live there, which is why I thought perhaps I had better try the west coast, which was supposed to be the beautiful bit.

I was made slightly nervous by the thought that they might all hate me for being English. Sydney Smith, clergyman and wit, writing in 1807 said, 'The great misfortune of Ireland is that the mass of the people have been given up for a century to a handful of Protestants by whom they have been treated as helots and subjected to every species of persecution and disgrace.'

To explain the remark I shall have to delve into another aspect of Irish history.

By way of preliminary, I wish to say that I find a great tendency for modern historians to go to some lengths to prove that the people who were there at the time, wherever or whenever it was, got it quite wrong when they wrote about it, whatever or whenever it may have been. This is quite understandable, as if the people who wrote at the time are supposed to have got it right, there would be nothing for modern historians to do. This is particularly true of professors of ancient history, because there are so few original sources. If the great Greek historians Herodotus, Thucydides and Xenophon were presumed to be right in what they tell us, then there would be no reason for today's historians to do anything more than repeat again and again what the ancients have told us already. As this would give the moderns no scope for the exercise of their own ingenuity, they devote themselves to showing, either in minute detail or in more general ways, that, after a lapse of some 2,500 years, they themselves know more than Herodotus, Thucydides and Xenophon about what actually happened. This they do by making a sort of jigsaw out of inscriptions on pieces of rock, bits of pottery, scraps culled either from other ancient writers such as poets, or from the works of later authors writing in Greek or Latin, plus a free use of their own imaginations, with a dash of speculation. All is underpinned by meticulous footnotes referring to the books and learned articles published by other modern writers who have made their own jigsaws at different times. Of course they may very well be right in what they say, and anyway it does no harm but keeps the pot of ancient history upon the boil.

I mention this only because I detect a tendency, in some modern historians that I have looked at, to argue that the sufferings of the Irish were not as bad as has often been made out. I propose to ignore all modern authors and rely upon two contemporary writers, Arthur Young, writing between 1777 and 1779, and Sydney Smith, writing in 1807.

By an Act of Parliament in England, only Protestants might sit in the Irish parliament, although Roman Catholics made up four fifths of the population. The 'Penal Laws' is the name generally given to that collection of vindictive legislation passed by the Irish Parliament against the Catholics. Arthur Young, who I have quoted before, tells us that 'the great category of persecuting laws (was introduced) six or seven years after the death of King William'. William III died in 1702, and the Penal Laws actually came into effect by degrees from 1707. When Sydney Smith in 1807 talks of the Irish 'being given up for a century to a handful of Protestants' he is talking of the century immediately before the period at which he was writing.

Sydney Smith is a man who will not fit neatly into any particular category, unless it be as one of the wittiest of satirical writers in the English language. He was a clergyman of the Church of England and absolutely not a friend to Roman Catholicism. 'We have not the slightest partiality for the Catholic religion; quite the contrary,' he says, using the authorial 'we' that was proper at the time. He had, notwithstanding, a burning aversion to all forms of injustice, and in consequence a passionate sympathy for the Catholic people of Ireland: 'Whatever your opinion may be of the follies of the Roman Catholic religion, remember that they are follies of four million human beings.' He was one of the founders of the greatly influential Edinburgh Review, in the pages of which he exercised his wit and talents in many ways, and particularly in the cause of the Irish Catholics, making for himself a good many enemies in the higher reaches of the Church of England as a result.

Arthur Young and Sydney Smith gave a similar, but not identical, description of the Penal Laws at their worst, and I will quote first from Sydney Smith:

No Catholic was to marry a Protestant, and any Catholic who sent a son to Catholic countries for education was to forfeit all his lands. In the reign of Queen Anne, any son of a Catholic who chose to turn Protestant got possession of his father's estate. No papist was allowed to purchase freehold property, or to take a lease of more than 30 years. If a Protestant dies intestate, the estate is to go to the next Protestant heir; if a Catholic dies intestate his estate is to go to the next Protestant. No papist is to dwell in Limerick or Galway. Prices of catching Catholic priests from fifty shillings to ten pounds according to rank. Papists are to answer all questions respecting all other papists, or to be committed to jail for twelve months.

In the reign of George II four-sixths of the population were cut off from the right of voting at elections. Persons robbed by privateers during a war with a Catholic state are to be indemnified by a levy on the Catholic inhabitants of the neighbourhood. All marriages between Catholics and Protestants are annulled. All popish priests celebrating them are to be hanged.

Arthur Young in his account adds that 'The laws of discovery, as they are called (require) priests who celebrate mass to be transported, and if they return to be hanged.

A Catholic having a horse in possession above the value of five pounds, to forfeit the same to the discoverer.' In effect this meant that any Protestant could offer a Catholic five pounds for his horse, and the offer could not be refused.

Taken as a whole, says Young, 'the system pursued in Ireland has had no other tendency but that of driving out of the kingdom all the personal wealth of the Catholics, and prohibiting their industry within it. The face of the country, every object in short which presents itself to the eye of a traveller, tells him how effectually this has been done. Those laws have crushed all the industry, and wrested most of the property from the Catholics; but religion triumphs; it is thought to increase.'

Religion did indeed triumph, owing to the pertinacity of the Irish people and the Irish priesthood, and even before the middle of the eighteenth century the laws restricting the exercise of the Catholic religion were virtually obsolete. Many, but not all, of the remaining penal laws were relaxed towards the end of the eighteenth century. 'Papists' now became 'His Majesty's Catholic subjects'. The right to vote at elections was restored; Protestants might marry Catholics provided the ceremony was conducted by a Protestant clergyman; Catholics might teach in schools. Among the remaining restrictions, Sydney Smith reserved his special scorn for the practice of compelling Irish Catholics to pay tithes for the support of the Protestant Episcopal Church of Ireland. Only a quarter of the population were Protestants, and half of these were Dissenters with no interest in the Episcopal Church whatever, and yet every Irish peasant, as well as paying rent to the middleman, had also to pay tithes to the Protestant clergyman, and would then contribute what he could to support the priest of his own religion.

'I submit to your common sense,' says Sydney Smith, 'if it be possible to explain to an Irish peasant upon what principle of justice, or common sense, he is to pay every tenth potato in his little garden to a clergyman in whose religion nobody believes for twenty miles around him, and who has nothing to preach to but bare walls.

'I admit that nothing can be more reasonable that to expect that a Catholic priest should starve to death, genteelly and pleasantly, for the good of the Protestant religion; but is it equally reasonable to expect that he should do so for Protestant brick and mortar? On an Irish Sabbath, the bell of a neat parish church often summons to church only the parson and an occasionally conforming clerk; while, two hundred yards off, a thousand Catholics are huddled together in a miserable hovel, and pelted by all the storms of heaven. Can any thing be more distressing than to see a venerable man pouring forth sublime truths in tattered breeches, and depending for his food upon the little offal he gets from his parishioners?'

His last word on the subject, found among his papers after his death was this:

> I have always compared the Protestant church in Ireland to the institution of butchers' shops in all the villages of our Indian empire. 'We will have a butcher's shop in every village, and you, Hindoos, shall pay for it. We know that many of you do not eat meat at all, and that the sight of beef steaks is particularly offensive to you; but still, a stray European may pass through your village, and want a steak or a chop: the shop *shall* be established; and you shall pay for it.' This is English legislation for Ireland!! There is no abuse like it in all Europe, in all Asia, in all the discovered parts of Africa, and in all we have heard of Timbuctoo!

Irish history does, of course, provide plenty more examples of injustice and misgovernment, but by introducing Captain Boycott, Arthur Young and Sydney Smith I have at least highlighted the two great issues of land and religion which dominate much of Irish history. I will just add a remark of Thomas Moore, the friend and biographer of the poet Lord Byron and himself a Catholic Irishman: 'My unlucky countrymen,' he says 'have always had a taste for justice – a taste as inconvenient to them, situated as they have always been, as a taste for horse-racing would be to a Venetian.'

All this was long in the past when I arrived on my bicycle. In Northern Ireland we were doing our best to be as nice as possible to absolutely every-one, including some very nasty people. However, pleasant as you may be later on you cannot treat people like helots for centuries without their hating you, and even if you leave off treating them like helots and they become an independent country, it is quite unreasonable to expect them to stop hating you. Except, of course, if they are Irish, when they cannot be expected to conform to any rule, and I was quite wrong to have had any anxiety. I met no trace of hostility anywhere barring the unpleasant man in my Dublin hotel. One of the landladies with whom I stayed said that while Germans were the most common visitors, the English were the least common, and she could not understand it. If it was a fear of hostile Irishmen that was keeping people away, I found no grounds for it whatever.

THE SECOND TRIP – CLARE AND GALWAY

To plan my second trip I rang the Irish Tourist Board to ask for some maps and guides, and was put through to Katrina Flanagan, who had such a lovely voice that it was a pleasure to hear it and I spun out the conversation for as long as I could. Talking to Katrina Flanagan is enough to make anyone want to go to Ireland at once, and she was so extremely helpful as well as entrancing to listen to that I asked if there was anything I could do for her in Ireland, and she said I was to send her a postcard from County Clare, which is where she comes from.

I had arranged to fly to Shannon and Aer Lingus had said that I would have to take the pedals off my bicycle, turn the handlebars sideways, remove the front wheel and pay for it all as excess baggage. When it came to the point I did not have to do any of those things, I just had to let the tyres down. This itself was a worry, as one of the recent technological advances had been for someone to invent tyres with a liquid in them that seals up holes with instant effect so that you never get punctures. Such tyres had been fitted by the bicycle shop but the liquid leaked all over my fingers when I let them down, leaving me to wonder whether they were still self-sealing or not. The next month illustrated the difficulty of proving the negative. I got no flat tyres, but whether this was because I got no punctures or whether I got punctures which were immediately sealed is one of those things I shall never know.

I had forgotten the Irish habit of saying 'How are you?' to complete strangers, but it extends to the Aer Lingus cabin staff and by the time I reached my seat at the back of the plane three different air hostesses had asked after my health. From where I sat I could see the baggage being loaded and two men arrived with a big, flat cardboard package labelled 'Bicycle. Fragile.' I was pretty impressed that it should have been done up so carefully but not by the difficulty they had in getting it on board. It behaved like a horse that did not want to go into a horsebox as it simply refused to go up the ramp. They heaved it this way and that without paying the least attention to the word 'fragile'. They dumped it on its end a couple of times in a savage manner, then at one moment walked away as if they had given the whole thing up as a bad job. I was about to ring for the air hostess and insist that the plane should not take off without my bicycle when they sneaked back and tried once more, this time with success. I sat back relieved, only to see my own Raleigh appear, not packed in cardboard at all, but just wheeled along as it was. It went in so easily that I felt quite proud of it.

I had planned this trip with pretty good care. On the last occasion the furthest I had got from Cork was Leenane, about 50 miles north-west of Galway. This time I meant to go on and follow the coast, more or less, all the way north to the border in County Donegal. After that I would put my bicycle on a bus or train to Dublin, in order to take a better look at a city which everyone told me, with one voice, that I had misjudged. They also made irritating remarks such as 'Did you go round the Dingle peninsula? You didn't? Oh dear!' Or 'Isn't the Ring of Kerry wonderful? What, you didn't go there?' They generally implied, in their condescending way, that I had hardly been anywhere worthwhile because I had missed out the one or two places which they themselves happened to have been to. Well, I wasn't having that, so after Dublin I would come back and circle the Dingle, as it seemed to be called, and the Ring of Kerry, and take in one or two other places that I was confident they had not visited, so that I could condescend to them in turn, especially as I would have done it by bicycle and they by some inferior means such as a car.

The nearest place from which to pick up from

where I left off before was Shannon, hence my decision to fly there. I set aside the month of June for the expedition and I filled my notebook with details of the route I meant to take and things I should see, gleaned from my pre-war guidebook, a couple of even older works such as Murray's *Handbook for Ireland* of 1864, the new *Blue Guide* to Ireland, all supplemented from the copious information supplied by the excellent Katrina Flanagan. I had a special reason for all this careful planning, in that the BBC Radio people had decided to take a hand in the proceedings.

They rang me out of the blue and said, 'Are you going anywhere?

'Such as where?' said I, rather surprised.

'Oh well, anywhere,' came the reply and I got the impression that they did not much care where I went as long as I went somewhere. Chicago perhaps or Alaska, or Baghdad.

'Yes,' I said, 'I'm going to Ireland on my bicycle.'

'Good,' they said. 'That will do nicely. Take a lightweight portable tape recorder and get some pieces about Ireland from which we can make a programme.'

A few days later a girl arrived by car and lugged into the house a great unwieldy tape recorder which had a long thick wire sticking out of it with the microphone at the end. She showed me how to work it, which would have been quite simple except that a few days into the expedition it started to go wrong, and later ceased to work at all. The girl herself went away and got another job, as I discovered when I came back with the tapes that I had managed to make by one means and another. (The first girl having disappeared, these tapes were then dumped on quite a different girl to make of them what she could.) As the supposedly light tape recorder was both heavy and bulky I had to buy a special extra carrier for my bicycle to accommodate it. With the recorder went an obligation to find some interesting people to talk to along the way, so that I could record what they said, and for help with this I rang my friend Marie Louise in Dublin.

To call her my friend at this stage is really premature, as we had been in each other's company for about half an hour in a radio studio, which hardly constitutes a lasting friendship. They were making a pilot programme for a series to be called *What's New?* and they had a very good reason for sending for Marie Louise, she being a quick, amusing and experienced Irish journalist and just the sort of person to liven up a programme. There was another girl, whose name I have rather rudely forgotten, and me, who at the age of 62 or thereabouts was hardly what you would normally call new. I had never been on the radio but had just started writing my column in The Oldie magazine, so perhaps I was new in an antiquated sort of way. My only recollection of the programme is that, during the discussion I thought of a joke of such appalling coarseness that I could not possibly make it but I wrote it on a piece of paper and passed it as a private communication to Marie Louise, who seemed to be an uninhibited sort of person. This she proved to be because she then read the joke out aloud and I think between us we must have wrecked the whole programme as it was never broadcast.

Now, about two years later, I tracked her down via the BBC and wrote to her in Dublin to tell her what I was up to. Back she came with a list of people I should look out for and her own phone number, so that we could meet in Dublin.

They gave me back my bicycle at Shannon but they had twisted it up somehow and jammed the front wheel so that it would not revolve. I could not get it to work, but the bicycle in the cardboard box which had given such trouble at take-off proved to belong to an American lady who understood these things better than I, and she fixed it. I set off in perfect cycling weather, once again through rolling countryside on a minor road to Sixmilebridge and Quin, to which one goes in order to take in the ruined Franciscan Abbey. It is in very good condition for a ruin, the cloisters being almost perfect. Here and at other Irish ruins I found that although the buildings were out of use they still keep burying people in the grave-yard, which gives a kind of continuity to the whole. I climbed a flight of stairs and found, by way of an agreeable surprise, some lawns. Lawns in my previous experience had always been on the ground floor, but here they were up on the first floor. I was definitely above ground because there were some railings to stop me falling off the lawn onto the earth below, and while leaning on these I found I was looking down on a party of Germans. This was also quite an agreeable sensation, not because I look down upon Germans in any figurative sense, but because I dislike travelling in an organised party and I felt superior at being alone.

From Quin my target was Ennistymon, passing through the town of Ennis, which Murray's 1864 guide described as 'a queer little town with narrow streets filled with a bustling foreign-looking people', though they didn't look particularly foreign or bustling to me. In 1864 there was, says Murray, 'a column erected to the memory of Daniel O'Connell, the Great Liberator. A statue is to be placed on the summit as soon as the money to pay for it is forthcoming – rather a doubtful event, to judge by the present lack of enthusiasm throughout the country.' I did not pause long enough to explore Ennis properly, but I am pleased to report that there is a figure of the Great Liberator on the top of the column, in spite of Murray's gloomy prognostication.

And so there should be. It was Daniel O'Connell, himself a Catholic, who successfully fought for the cause of Emancipation, culminating in the Catholic Emancipation Act of 1829. This Act allowed Roman

Catholics to sit in Parliament, and made them eligible for senior posts in the Army, the Navy, the Law, and, with a couple of exceptions, in government. O'Connell wrung this from the reluctant Duke of Wellington, then Prime Minister, and from the equally reluctant Sir Robert Peel, then Leader of the Commons, and from the even more reluctant George IV, who thought it conflicted with his obligation under his Coronation Oath to maintain the Protestant religion.

O'Connell later campaigned, this time unsuccessfully, for the repeal of the Act of Union of 1800 which had abolished the Irish Parliament and given Ireland similar status to Scotland. Although his methods were entirely peaceful he was charged, along with eight others, with creating disorder and disaffection and was convicted by a packed jury. The government's first step towards securing a conviction was to contrive to lose the names of 67 Catholics from the list of potential jurors. From this truncated list, 48 were chosen by lot, to form a pool from which the final 12 were to come. Of the 48, 11 were Catholics, and as both sides had the right to object to 12 names, the Crown was able to strike them all out and make sure of a wholly Protestant jury.

T. B. Macaulay, later Lord Macaulay, speaking in the House of Commons, said the verdict was obtained with the help of a Chief Justice of whose charge to the jury 'I can hardly bring myself to speak. It bears a very close resemblance to some charges which may be found in the state trials of the reign of Charles the Second.' The conviction was finally quashed in the House of Lords by a majority of three to two, the judges dividing on political lines, Liberals against Tories, and O'Connell was released after spending three months in Richmond Jail. This marked the effective end of O'Connell's political career, and I tell the story at some length to show the dangers of standing up to the established powers in England on behalf of Ireland as late as 1843. That there could really have been no enthusiasm for a statue, as Murray suggests, seems almost incredible.

From Ennis I passed on to Ennistymon, this being my first place to spend the night, according to my master plan. Unpacking my bag in an eminently comfortable ITB Approved room after an interval of two years felt just like coming home. To show the immense benefit conferred upon travelling humanity by the Irish Tourist Board, let me tell you how things were in County Clare in 1890, according to a French lady called Madame de Bovet: 'The English bed, whose bad reputation is fully justified, is a paradise by the side of an Irish bed. What the under-mattress is made of I have never been able to make out. One thing is certain – that it contains nothing even approaching to elasticity. On this hard basis are one or two thin mattresses, very tightly stuffed with something that resembles peach stones.' In those days there were bell-pulls in the bedrooms but, says Madame de Bovet, 'You might as well ring your bell in the desert. "It does not matter," says the maid good temperedly, "there is no bell." And when, in a fresh access of rage you say, "Then one might die in this room without any means of making oneself heard?" your mouth is shut by the girl's sublime answer "Oh! That has *never* happened!"'

Ennistymon is a little town on the Inagh River, which river is crossed by a stone bridge with seven arches and which splashes over some flat rocks to make a pretty good waterfall. The BBC girl had told me that I must get some wildtracks which she explained were general background sounds and effects to provide a bit of Irish atmosphere, so I made a wildtrack of the Ennistymon water-fall. I have since discovered that wildtracks are very popular with the men who record the sound for television programmes. Every now and then the sound recordist will demand absolute silence and we all sit as quiet as mice while he waves a furry boom around. These wildtracks never seem to play a noticeable part in the programme when it comes to be made, and I doubt if they are ever much use, which was certainly the case with my Ennistymon waterfall wildtrack. Rushing water in Ennistymon sounds the same as rushing water anywhere else, and you could make a recording of running bathwater and pass it off as a water-fall if you felt like it.

Ennistymon, along with Doolin and Lahinch, is said to be a centre of Irish music, particularly flute music, and flute music would have made an altogether better wildtrack than a waterfall. I had hopes of getting a bit of fluting onto tape, but it was not so much for this that I had come to Ennistymon, but to seek out a man called Willie Daley, who is a matchmaker. By this I mean that he is a bringer together of men and women with a view to matrimony, not a manufacturer of Swan Vestas in his garage, or running a subsidiary of Bryant & May. That I should talk to him was one of the tips I got from Marie Louise.

Everyone in Ennistymon knows Willie Daley. I had only to mention to my landlady that I hoped to meet him for her to send me at once to a pub where she said I was bound to find him. It proved to be a long dingy bar with one sign outside saying 'Guinness' and another saying 'Matrimonial Shack'. Inside was a ghetto blaster blasting out Irish jigs, with a further sign beside it saying 'Live Music'. There was no Willie Daley, but a nice girl behind the bar said that he might be in and he might not, and that I could ring him at home if I liked. She gave me his number, probably thinking that I was in need of a wife, but he wasn't at home. Whoever answered the phone agreed with the idea that he might turn up at the Matrimonial Shack and he might not, but if he didn't I should ring in the morning. I went back to eat fish and chips beside the ghetto blaster, hoping that Live Music might arrive equipped with flutes, but not a single flautist turned up. The only other people in the bar were two Welsh girls who said they were hoping for music, but I suspect they were really hoping for husbands. Whichever it was, they stayed on and I went off to bed.

Willie Daley was at home next morning, and invited me in a most friendly way to meet him at his pony-trekking place. I arrived a bit early at what I thought was the right farm, to be welcomed by three young greyhounds and a couple of Shetland ponies but no people as the place was deserted. Eventually I looked through the window of the house to find that it seemed to have been abandoned altogether. I further noticed that the greyhounds were just as much at home in another house two hundred yards away, so I went there and Willie Daley's young son came rushing out to say that his father was not yet home but I was to come in for a cup of tea.

Willie arrived before the kettle had boiled, only to hurry off again with his son to attend to some pony-trekkers. He delegated the tea-making to his daughter, who was a delightful girl about to go to college to learn to be a chef with a view she said, to setting up an Irish bar in some foreign part such as Greece. It seemed a startling ambition that showed great initiative, so I wished her every success.

'Is there much going on in the match-making line?' I asked as we waited for the kettle.

'All the time,' she said. 'They ring up at two in the morning from America. "Willie," they say, "have you found me a husband yet?"'

I was quite happy sitting there because County Clare is very beautiful and we were high up with a panorama of rocks and hills, plus a glimpse of the sea at Lehinch. Willie, when he came back, pointed out three prehistoric hill forts which could be seen from his kitchen, each a kind of grassy basin perhaps sixty to a hundred yards in diameter.

A nicer, more benevolent man than Willie himself would be hard to find. He had a greying beard, piercing blue eyes and a soft voice. The pony-trekkers had wanted to go to the Haunted House. 'What Haunted House?' I asked.

'It's an old house now, originally it was a landlord's house. There were two hangings in it and they were both done on the evening of a wedding. The woman was a landlord's daughter, she was a good age but she was attractive. I remember her myself when I was four or five and she was a lovely person but she was getting on a bit all right.

'Now she kind of chose the men she wanted to marry and it was assumed that they might not have liked her, and rather than go through with it that was reason of the hangings. Later it was found that there was a man, he was from Holland, that worked with her as a kind of gardener-cum-friend like, maybe a close friend at a point of time. He was a big tall man with blonde fair head of hair and your man's name was Hands. My mother used visit them and they would come to our house for tea and she would go down to them. But the hard part of it was this, that my mother would be getting their tea and she would say to my two sisters and me, "Will you go and tell Hands to come in for his tea?" and we used be really embarrassed because he'd only one arm. We'd be shouting "Hands, Hands" and we used say "Jesus you'd think they would get a better name than Hands for a man with only one arm!" It was only in the latter years that we found out that H-A-N-S was his name.

'But it was found out at the last instant,' said Willie, 'that it was actually he that had done both cases.' There he paused. I took him to mean, by what he had said, that somehow the one-armed Hans had contrived to hang the two would-be bridegrooms, but there was that in Willie's manner which suggested that he would not like to say any more than he had. So I nodded. 'What then?' I asked.

'They left at that stage and that is nearly fifty years ago. That house below is a huge house with a lovely gate entrance, main house, coach houses and a total enclosure of trees. Since I've grown up from my early years it's called the Haunted

House, and myself I'd be very nervous passing it by night for we that grew up in the area have been taught an awful amount of ghost stories.'

I asked what had set him going as a matchmaker, and he said he had started because he had a lot of neighbours in their mid forties and fifties who weren't getting married. 'They were getting older and sometimes dying off maybe at a point of time. Very often they would be grand, these bachelors, as long as their father and mother would still be alive, but as soon as they'd die off, they'd get old pretty quickly and get into disrepair. Eventually their houses would be sold off to people all over the world, and I felt I was losing great neighbours and great friends so it's based on that that I started.

'There were not ever too many women in this area, unfortunately, no. When I was growing up myself I remember going to a dance and there would be eleven fellows to each woman. This is a serious matter that would happen, that you'd go across the floor to ask a girl to dance and she could say "No" and there would be at least ten other fellows behind your back. Now I saw in a farming magazine that there is twenty-nine-and-a-half fellows to every woman west of the Shannon.'

The more we talked, (or rather the more he talked, for I did little more than give the conversation a nudge from time to time) the more I felt that, like a minor J. M. Synge, I was recording a way of life and a style of speech that would soon be in the past. I hope not. I hope that in beautiful and remote areas such as this part of County Clare, the lovely flowing cadences in which Willie spoke will somehow survive the onslaught of multiple channels of foreign television and the globalisation of everything. I fear they may not, but for the present it was a pure pleasure to listen to this prince of raconteurs as he told me of his first experience of a match being made.

'This fellow liked this girl but the father was very hard to know and a bit of a cross man. He was a nice man but he sounded as if he was cross and your man was a bit afraid to make the approach. Then he saw this day that he had a pig for sale, a fat pig, it was in the papers. So he says to me, "Will you come with me Willie? You might be able to give me a hand."

'I hadn't started matchmaking at this stage but I had been a witness when I was eleven at a match being made. In those particular years it was called "plucking the gander". Now I went with him and I was kind of shy myself because I was half afraid of this man, but we went in and saw himself. He came out and his daughter came out and she was a very, very good-looking girl. She'd a beautiful head of black hair and a lovely white skin, a really beautiful girl. So he was asking twenty-seven pounds for the pig and you judge a pig by the back. Himself he turned around and pressed his hands on the pig and "That's a good pig," he said, "that pig was well fed." And your man the young lad that was the buyer: "Ah, he could be better," he says, "he's a bit soft in the back." So the young girl at that stage: "He is not!" she says. "I fed that pig. He'd fine meal, oats and barley. That is a good pig!" she says. And your man turns around and he says, "Will you eat him with me then? Will you eat him with me?" For that was the only chance he could get. So they developed from that and inside of a few months they got married and they're quite happy people enough you know.'

I had supposed that most of those who applied to him were the sort of local bachelor that he had described, but it is not so. Lots of girls come from America, he told me, to find husbands in Ireland.

'Lovely people, very attractive girls, though last year they were very, very orientated-looking, they looked like they were forth from some oriental place. They'd be very youngish looking with their big heads of hair but you'd know there would be other parts of them not as young looking as that. They come to Lisdoonvarna six miles up the road – it's only a small place, a little village and when you get out of one door you'd be into any other door inside of half a minute. They come for the whole month of September – there's music in about ten places and they dance all bloody day, all evening and all night. It's a great opportunity for people to meet.'

I asked how he would provide for me if I came looking for a wife. Taking note of my obvious age he said, 'I'll tell you an interesting story now. Valentine's Day brings out a whole burst of emotions out of people that might have lain dormant for a year. A man rang me a week before Valentine's Day a year ago, he was eighty-three years of age, and he said to me about meeting someone. When I got back to him (it took me about a month,) he said, "Look Willie, I think I'm going to give it a miss." So I says, "Fair enough, fair enough."

'Now he rang me again this year, five times in the one week at very irregular hours. I'd a cow calving one night and the ropes round the legs of the calf and my son helping me all right and I thought, 'Jesus you'd think he'd pick his time a bit better.' He came over to this house to me and I said, 'Did you ever think about doing this before?"

'I didn't,' he says. 'I thought of it last year.'

'When you were fifty or sixty did you ever consider it?'

'No,' he said, 'my mother and father lived to be over ninety when they both died and we were very happy.'

'Were you ever out with a woman before?' I asked, in the course of a good conversation like, for I didn't bring the questions out directly like that. 'No,' he said, and I said to myself, 'Isn't that a lovely thing that he got that notion at that age?'

'I introduced him to a woman who rang me from thirty miles away. She told me a bit about herself and she said, 'Willie, could you get me someone slightly retired? I don't want an ambitious person, I just want someone I can enjoy with and relax with."

'There is a man now,' I said, 'has a similar interest. He's semi-retired, he's a farmer, but he's a fair good age. He's hitting around eighty.'

'I'd like someone like that,' she said.

'Now this was a funny situation. She was thirty-eight and an attractive girl definitely. I collected her when I was introducing them and she'd nice dark hair and a lovely red costume, black tights on her and a mini skirt and she looked very gorgeous. So we were talking as we went along and I was saying to myself, 'Jesus, if he don't turn up I might have a night out myself.'

'So we walked into the lounge where I had arranged to meet the man, and he was sitting there, a very timid little man, I'd be honest about it, very shy. I got them a drink and he took out a fiver and she was drinking brandy and port and he wasn't drinking at all. So she took over, she was a great conversationalist, and he was kind of good after a while. Anyway I made a phone call, I'd a mare that was close to foaling and I said to them, 'Excuse me now, I'll be back to you in a minute.' As soon as I got back she says to me, "Willie, if you like you can go away now, for John is making arrangements for me go get home."'

I said in a trite sort of way, that if he could make such a satisfactory introduction between a fellow hitting 83 and a beautiful woman of 38 there seemed to be no limit to what he could achieve.

'Well,' said Willie reflectively, 'there's no old shoe without a stocking to fit it, but there has to be some magic in it between them. All my life I've said you have to have about sixty per cent of magic and just some start to it, to begin with.'

This, I think, put his whole philosophy of affairs of the heart into a nutshell. It seemed the right moment for me to depart, as I had taken up a good deal of his time. For all I knew there might be pony-trekkers waiting or cows calving, all needing his attention, but I think he was too hospitable even to give a hint if such was the case. I shook hands with Willie and with his daughter, wishing her success with her Irish bar in Greece, and rode off in a most satisfactory frame of mind, delighted at having encountered so benevolent a person doing so much good for his fellow men and his fellow women.

Willie set me off on a tiny peaceful road to Kilfenora, on which I met two cars in half an hour. Kilfenora used to be a Bishopric but the Pope 'at a point of time', as Willie would say, wanted to demote it and bring it under the See of Galway. To this insult the people of Kilfenora objected so violently that His Holiness was obliged to compromise the matter by saying he would be Bishop of Kilfenora himself, and he still is. The Pope is the Bishop of Kilfenora and the Bishop of Galway in his Apostolic Administrator.

This I learned at the Burren Centre at Kilfenora, where there is an admirable display from which I gathered most of my information about the botanical aspects of the Burren. It should not be missed by anyone passing by. This centre is, I think, the main feature of Kilfenora, and the only sign of its papal dignity is a small church which was once the cathedral.

It came on to rain at Kilfenora, starting as what used to be called 'light rain or drizzle' but which the grinning Welsh girl on television now calls 'spits and spots of rain'. Later it turned into serious rain but it did not seem to matter much. My top was dry and my legs wet and I was fine. I passed by Lemenagh Castle, which was built by Máire Ruadh O'Brien and her husband Conor but captured by Ludlow, Cromwell's general, in the course of which action Conor was killed. Máire Ruadh undertook to marry one of Ludlow's soldiers in order to keep her land and Cornet Cooper was the lucky man, but she murdered him later by pushing him out of a window so I suppose there was no magic in it. Now the castle is just a ruined façade belonging to a Peter O'Brien who

117

does not want you to trespass and has put up two notices and an electric fence to enforce his wishes.

I was now cycling through the Burren for the second time in my life but on an inland rather than coastal route, past small fields with great outcrops of rock. It is an area of prehistoric habitation which the older guidebooks describe as wild and lonely. This was before the advent of Greimann Reisen of Bremen, widely celebrated for his huge green and yellow charabancs which descend on lonely parts of the globe and disgorge quantities of his countrymen.

There was such a party swarming over the fields to visit a dolmen. After they had gone a solitary German drove up by car, and on what I believe to be the fixed Teutonic principle of seeing as little as possible of the country when abroad, he stayed in his seat and photographed the dolmen through a telescopic lens at a distance of 200 yards. The fact that he was alone perhaps made him feel nervous. The Greimann Reisenders had been in a crowd and probably felt safe in getting out of their bus as wherever they looked they saw someone else who was German, whereas he, being by himself, would have had no such re-assurance.

I stopped twice on the way to Ballyvaughan, first to look at a wedge tomb and then I joined a party to tour the Allwee Caves, a long natural tunnel going half a mile into the mountain and dimly lit

by electric light. We admired stalactites and stalag-
mites and the fifteen-hundred-year-old bones of
a brown bear which had come in to hibernate and
expired in its sleep. The guide had two rather good
tricks. At one point we could hear rushing water
which was invisible until he flipped a switch and
we saw a beautiful clear spout of water dropping
thirty or forty feet exactly on to a spotlight which
illuminated it all the way up. His other party piece
was to say 'You came here today to see a cave –
well, this is what it looks like!' and then put off
the lights, leaving the party shrieking in utter darkness. 'Good luck on the way out,' he says cheerily,
as if he had not made the joke twenty times already
that day. This causes more shrieking and laughter
and then he puts the light on and the visitors find
their way out.

I stayed that night at O'Brien's pub in
Ballyvaughan. When I reached it I found that I
had breached the first rule of cycling in Ireland,
which is 'Pack everything in a polythene bag', so
some of my things were pretty wet. I went out
that evening feeling hungry as well as damp, and
consulted the waiter at the Hylands Hotel about
the spare ribs available in the bar. 'Jesus,' he said,
'if you eat them you won't want to eat for a week,'
on which warm recommendation I had them, and
very good they were. It rained throughout the
night, and I wondered sleepily what the gurgling
noise was in the early hours, and found out when
I stepped into the bathroom in the morning,

because the drains had risen through the shower outlet and flooded the floor.

From Ballyvaughan, via Kintara, I struck off on an utterly peaceful cross-country road to Kilmacduagh. Just before the turning I stopped to send the promised postcard to Katrina Flanagan at the Irish Tourist Board in London.

The shop where I bought it was in the care of a small red-headed American girl who said she had lived in Ireland for five years.

'Are you married?' I asked, thinking to do her a good turn. 'Not yet,' she said. 'Well,' I began, 'I can recommend you to a really good matchmaker. His name is Willie Daley . . .'

'I live next door to Willie Daley,' she said, 'and come here every day by bus,' so that was the end of my good intentions.

As you enter Kilmacduagh there are on the left about seven almost identical white bungalows with manicured lawns as if straight from the Chelsea Flower Show, and on the right the ruins of seven ecclesiastical buildings including a cathedral, an Augustinian Priory and the finest Round Tower that you are ever likely to see. It all dates back to the seventh century when a monastery and Bishopric were founded by Saint Colman Macduagh, otherwise Colman son of Duagh.

In the graveyard there was an old gentleman holding a saw who explained to me about the

Round Tower. It leans two feet out of the upright and must, he said, have been built like that as if it had moved two feet by itself it would inevitably have fallen over.

'That is the Tower of Kilmacduagh – 'tis one-hundred-and-twelve feet high and the monks put it up. When the Vikings were coming they rang the bell in the old cathedral and the people went into the Tower and brought all their valuables in. All the gold chalices and all the symbodiums, they took them all in with them. The first door was forty-seven feet from the ground and they got up in a rope ladder. There are several rooms inside and they went from one room to the next in ladders. You will see on every door that is there the marks of their boots. That is where the rope ladder came near to the door, and there is some at one hundred feet, right up to the very top, and their boots came against the Tower and those marks are the proof of it.' He made it a most vivid scene, and in spite of not knowing what he meant by a symbodium, I could in my mind's eye see the people scrambling up the rope ladders, scrabbling against the walls with their boots, and then gazing fearfully down on the Vikings below.

'We did have seven Roman Catholic Churches here. There was colleges here, there was schools here; they came from Europe here to school, from France and all over in those days. They started in the sixth century and they came here in the fourteenth, the fifteenth and the sixteenth centuries. So then Cromwell came along and he burned them down and that is what is left of them there.'

I asked if they got many visitors now, for at the time there was no one else around.

'We do,' he said. 'We get a lot of Americans and Australians, we get a lot from France and Germany and Switzerland. Oh 'tis worth coming here, 'tis worth coming here!' he said, and so it is, for it is a fine romantic site with the magnificent hills of the Burren as a background to it all.

From Kilmacduagh I made my way across country and for the second time in my life struggled into Galway in the teeth of a headwind on a busy main road in intermittent rain. This is a horrible experience which I hope never to repeat, and as there seems to be no other way into Galway I never want to go there again. Actually I never want to go to Galway again anyway, never mind the difficulty of getting there, but this is a sign that there is something wrong with me as everyone says it is a wonderful city and gets very cross if you say anything else. The only good thing that happened to me in it was that I rang up a cousin of my wife whom neither she nor I had ever met, and made an assignation with her through her daughter. She was not at all sure who I was or why I was there. 'How are you related to Deirdre?' she asked as I entered the flower shop where she works.

'Pretty closely,' said I, 'considering she is my

wife.' On that basis she shut the shop and we went out to dinner and a very good dinner it was.

Apart from her, Galway seemed to be full of much the same people as before, of whom a high percentage were drunks, dropouts, drug addicts or beggars. I was stopped in the street by a man who said, 'I've had bad luck with my car and I've no money for a drop of petrol.'

'Oh, let's see,' said I, fishing out my change.

'No, no,' he said, stopping me with a grand gesture. 'I'll not take money off you. But you could *lend* me ten pounds until I get some petrol?'

'No I couldn't.'

'Well, five pounds then?'

'No.'

'Well, what are you going to give me?'

'Nothing. You've missed your chance.'

This prepared me for an encounter next day when a van stopped me as I was cycling towards Maam Cross.

'Could you help me at all?'

'I rather doubt it,' I said, as I am no mechanic and would be no use if there was something wrong with the van.

'The van is almost out of petrol and the child is sick and I have to get to the hospital.' In token of proof he pointed first at a red light shining on the dashboard and then at a healthy-looking child sucking lustily at a bottle on its mother's lap.

'Let's see,' I said once more, dredging up my change.

'You'll need all that for yourself,' he said contemptuously, and drove off. Later that day as I cycled through a village the very same van came past me from behind and turned into a trim-looking house with a boat and a trailer in the garden. Begging on the grand scale is obviously profitable and all you need is a hungry baby and sufficient electrical skill to adapt the petrol warning light so that it comes on whenever you want.

I had my hair cut in Galway, making Ireland the ninth country in which I have undergone that operation at different times of my life. In a further effort to get wildtracks on my recorder I asked the girl haircutter if I could have the machine on while she snipped away, but she said she was too shy. The talk in Irish pubs they call 'the craic', only they pronounce it 'the crack' and it was just as well that I did not record the Irish barbershop craic as it was a non-stop recital of every detail of all the recent episodes of a television programme called *999*, and thoroughly dull.

After Galway it was a hard struggle again in the wind, which was blowing strongly from the west. I stopped before Oughterard to see Aughnanure Castle, formerly a stronghold of the O'Flahertys. 'A particularly ferocious family,' said the girl at the entrance, which accords with the inscription that used to be over the west gate of Galway: 'From the fury of the O'Flahertys Good Lord deliver us.' Aughnanure Castle, built in 1500, was their stronghold from which they terrorised the local populace and occasionally tangled with the English. The Castle is now a semi-renovated ruin with a square keep, trim lawns and fine views, but is not particularly interesting. This view I shared with an elderly couple from Wisconsin who were wondering why they had come so far to see so little.

As I puffed along after that a fit young Frenchman came alongside. I was pleased to find that he could not go any faster then me, although he could keep it up for longer because I stopped, exhausted, for tea at Maam Cross and he rode on to Clifden. He was a redundant computer man having a three-month break from work and his girlfriend, before looking for fresh employment and returning to her embraces. If he rode in front (and single file was safest as there was a bit of traffic,) he acted as a wind break and the cycling was easier, but for the honour of England I felt we had to take it in turns so I went in front for an equal share of the time.

They told me at Maam Cross that there was a bed-and-breakfast place three miles further on so I fought my way forward, devoutly hoping that this was so. The merit of Connemara, where I now was, is that it is extremely empty. There were long stretches of road in front of me with lakes, rocks and mountains but no sign of human habitation, a vista which would normally have been wholly delightful but which on this occasion would have been greatly embellished by a house with a B&B sign. Eventually one arrived, or at least the sign was there, the house being a good half-mile up a steep track. The girl who cut my hair in Galway had said that as it was a holiday weekend I needed to book ahead because everywhere would be full. As I toiled towards the house on the hill I wondered if it was a mirage which would melt away altogether as I arrived, or just a real house which would turn me away because it was full, but it was neither. A small girl of about eleven years old gave me permission to stay, showed me to my room, and asked if I wanted tea. The work of running these establishments is often entrusted to children, and various elves and urchins come and go with plates, ask you if you would like tea or coffee, and return halfway through breakfast to ask with punctilious politeness if everything is to your liking. You may not see an adult at all until it comes to the matter of parting with money.

It was a lovely spot looking over a lake which an elf informed me was Orid lake with, she said, Orid mountain beyond. (At least, that is what she seemed to say, but as I can find neither lake nor mountain on any map, perhaps she said something else.) I slept superbly, my diet this day having been the usual vast breakfast but then leek and potato soup for lunch, two scones for tea, and

126

three biscuits and a pot of tea for supper. Cholesterol poisoning seemed less likely than usual and I was not at all hungry.

The next day it rained from ten in the morning until late at night but I did not care at all because there was no wind. The bicycle loved it, bowling along as far as Roundstone like a fresh horse out hunting. If I had ridden it at a wall I do believe it would have jumped it. I turned off the main Clifden road, down what my 1938 ten-penny guidebook calls the 'Brandy and Soda Route' because the air is so exhilarating. The first stop was at Ballynahinch Castle, now a superior and expensive hotel much patronised by fishermen and Americans. Two of the latter were squabbling in the bar over the matter of her taking his photograph:

'I can't see through it, honey.'
'But I set it, honey.'
'I still can't see, honey.'
'Oh God damn it, you have altered the lens.'

Ballynahinch Castle belonged at one time to Mr Richard Martin MP, a friend of the Prince Regent and a noted duellist, for which reason he was known as 'Hairtrigger Dick'. Later in life he became keen on animal welfare and founded the RSPCA, so then they called him 'Humanity Dick'. There was no suggestion that any change came over his character, or that he found shooting his fellow men at all inconsistent with his being kind to animals. Ingenious nicknames run in the Martin family. There was an earlier Richard Martin who switched allegiance from James II to William III at the right moment, and was rewarded with a grant of all the O'Flaherty land in Galway, which feat earned him the nickname 'Nimble Dick'.

A benevolent elderly man who was lounging about swapping fishing stories in the bar insisted that I take a walk through the grounds beside the river and lake, so I did, and most beautiful it was. This particular part of Connemara must be superb walking country and you can buy guides at the Castle, so I resolved to come back with my wife when I am a millionaire, which you need to be to stay there. Then I rode on by the Brandy and Soda route, much exhilarated by the air, the woods and the little lakes beside the road, as far as Roundstone, where the gloomy prognostications of the Galway haircutter nearly came true. The first three places I tried were full, but I got a room at the fourth.

And I am glad the first three were full as the fourth was excellent. It was in a brick house up a flight of stairs, which was a distinction in itself, and had a particularly obliging landlady who was a very good cook and ready to feed me in the evening as well as at breakfast.

Roundstone itself is a pretty little fishing and lobster-catching village, with a harbour studded with little islands. My ancient Murray's guide tells me that it was at one time 'destined to fulfil a great purpose, no less than to be the starting-point from Ireland to America. For this end a good road was made to it, and a convenient pier built by Nimmo the engineer, who saw in the beautiful and capacious bay capabilities of no common order. But the course of events at Galway will most likely preclude the chance of Roundstone ever emerging from its obscurity.' Roundstone having thus lapsed into a state of comfortable nonentity in the shadow of Galway, I did not expect to find anyone to help me with a distressing problem with which I was now afflicted, but I was wrong.

The problem was with the BBC recording machine which had taken to making rotten recordings, with a version of what Lewis Carroll in *Through the Looking Glass* calls 'outgribing – something between bellowing and whistling, with a kind of a sneeze in the middle'. In this case it was something between a shriek and a quaver with a sort of squeal in the background.

I had tried to get through by telephone to the BBC girl who gave me the thing in the first place, to see if she could listen down the line and tell me what was wrong with it. This was almost an adventure in itself. The payphone gobbled up money so quickly that I tried unsuccessfully to reverse the charges. Then instead of a human being I got a user-hostile switchboard manned by a female Dalek who made mad remarks like 'if you know the extension you want, dial it.' When I finally got hold of a real person she was Irish, so naturally I thought she must be the Irish Telecom operator getting in on the act and not a BBC person at all. She did actually work for the BBC, and when at last we got down to business all I could establish was that neither this Irish BBC girl nor anyone else knew anything at all either about the girl I was trying to find or, indeed, about me.

So there I was, on my own and wandering disconsolately about Roundstone when I came upon a rustic/artistic industrial estate. The rustic element consisted of people such as sheepskin sellers selling sheepskin items, and the artistic element of potters selling pots, with a traditional Irish Musical Instrument maker selling drums. This caused me mild surprise, which was nothing compared to my delight at the industrial element, in the shape of a big modern building labelled 'Connemara Electronics'. It was shut as it was Sunday, and it would be shut on Monday which was a holiday, but I resolved to stay till Tuesday as it was altogether astonishing to find such a place in a fishing village in a far corner of Connemara, and I didn't expect to find another between here and Dublin.

I have spoken of Connemara as if everyone knows what area the name covers, but they may not. I should therefore explain that it is applied in general to the area between Galway Bay and Clew Bay, and in particular to the south-west part round Clifden. The east side does not seem to be clearly defined, but I think a line from Maam Cross to Westport is roughly the eastern limit. At Ballynahinch I had been just on the southern edge of what the map now designates the Connemara National Park. Whether this is a new idea, or whether such a park was in being when I passed through, I cannot say, but I certainly saw no signs to alert me to such a thing. Mr Piehler of the 1938 guidebook gets pretty lyrical about the 'austere beauty' of Connemara. 'A grey-green land of stony mountains, moors, and bogs, of a thousand loughs and streams, of bays, sea inlets, and sandy beaches, of picturesque cottages set among rocks, with their thatched roofs weighted down with stones – no traveller can fail to be impressed with its subtle colouring and alluring loveliness of form.' So he describes it, and I agree, except for the picturesque cottages with thatched roofs, which have either disappeared or been replaced by white bungalows. Never mind, these bungalows are a great improvement on the dreadful Irish 'cabins' such as those described by William Cobbett, whom I quoted earlier. Oliver Goldsmith says in his *History of Rome* that 'a dearth of historical occurrences is generally the happiness of the people.' In the same way one might say that 'an absence of the picturesque is generally the comfort of the occupants.'

★　　★　　★

Next morning I rested the bicycle and walked on what my landlady called the Island Walk between fuchsia hedges and over a small bridge onto the Island of Innishnee. This was grey and wet but striking, and I fell in with a goat which was stuck by the horns in a pig-wire fence like Abraham's ram in a thicket, so I released it. Then I met a countryman going to look after his cows. He gave me the impression that the place was full of house-boats.

'Are you a Yank?'

'No – English.'

'Ah, there's lots of Yanks here. Senator Dodd of America has a houseboat here.'

'Has he indeed?'

'He has. And Germans. There's plenty Germans has a houseboat here. There's a German has a houseboat *there*!' and he pointed at a small white cottage half a mile inland. This puzzled me a little until I realised he was saying 'a house bought' and not a houseboat. This was quite a relief as Roundstone appeared to be a genuine fishing village with eight or so fishing boats but no yachts, and I did not like the thought of flotillas of Yanks and Germans in houseboats. I must admire the Irish ingenuity. They get big subsidies out of the European Union, build little white bungalows with the proceeds and then sell them to Yanks and Germans. This might seem a dangerous proceeding as they could get over-run with foreigners, but the Irish dealt successfully in the end with the Vikings, the Normans and the English so I do not suppose a sprinkling of Americans and Germans will give them any trouble.

That evening the sun came out, the grey sea turned blue, I could see mountains from my window that I had not known were there and the great hill of Errisbeg made its appearance to tower above us. I went for a spin on the bicycle, the gorse fairly shining by the roadside, and by taking an unmarked turning I looped through a genuinely unspoilt fishing village with a jetty, boats, nets, lobster pots and no shops, pubs or B&B signs, just cottages. It is spelt Erralagh, though how you pronounce it is another matter entirely.

All about Roundstone there were signs saying 'Save the Sea Trout' so being always ready to help in an emergency I asked my landlady what was up.

'There are some who say it is the lice from the salmon farms are eating the sea trout alive but my father who is a fisherman says that is all nonsense. It has happened before and will happen again that the sea trout go up and down in number, and that is what is happening now.' Whatever the reason I could see the problem was serious because they gave me a leaflet at Hairtrigger Dick's castle which showed the sea trout catch had been 1,504 in 1987, fell to 20 in 1989, and since then had been a matter of 'catch and release'. If expensive fishing was reduced to the level of hauling fish out of the water

133

and throwing them back as if they were mere perch or dace in a pond, things had come to a pretty pass.

That evening I dined on a first-rate salmon steak which my landlady served up, and read a book which she lent me. The salmon steak was the result of a discussion with my landlady who had made up her mind that I needed building up after all my cycling, and was wondering whether it would be more effective to feed me on beef steak or salmon steak. In my opinion there is no beating beef at its best, but getting it at its best is really difficult, so I played safe and went for the salmon, which was memorably delicious. The book was called *The Master*. It was the autobiography of a school teacher and the *Irish Press* said it had 'a touch of genuine magic' and the *Sunday Tribune* that it was 'elegantly written and stylish'. I have already made plain my admiration for Irish writers in general and pass no opinion on this one in particular, but will quote a conversation between the author and his lifelong friend Ned. The passage goes like this, Ned speaking first:

> 'Got my walking papers today.'
> 'What do you mean?'
> 'Results of the biopsy,' he said. 'I've got the Big C.'
> I was thunderstruck. I paused. 'Hell Ned,' I said, 'you'll beat that rap!'

Whether this should be described as elegant and stylish is a point which I leave to the reader.

The next day, although it was a Tuesday, Connemara Electronics remained obstinately shut and a patriarch with a broom who was sweeping up leaves said they would not open until tomorrow. This was not the disaster that it seemed to be as he had the answer: 'Jackie Ward in Clifden. Jackie Ward can fix anything.' So I took the coast road to Clifden, a brief exhilarating spin on the Brandy and Soda route, and found Jackie Ward's place. There a man said the batteries were flat in my machine, tested the batteries, found they were not and said: 'I'll get one of my engineers to fix it. Give it half an hour.' To find in the heart of the generally empty and barren Connemara an establishment with a body of electrical engineers any one of whom was capable of fixing a BBC recording machine in half an hour was a very surprising thing. It was the case however, as in half an hour I got it back and it was not outgribing at all, so the recording enterprise which I had just about written off as hopeless was now revived.

On the way into Clifden I had exchanged waves with three shaven-headed figures in long brown robes and sandals, carrying huge backpacks and walking along the road in single file like ducks. Now I found them standing in the broad main street collecting food in bowls, or so they hoped, though business did not seem very brisk. They were on a pilgrimage which they seemed to call 'Tu-dong', to Croagh Patrick, the holy mountain in County Mayo. They were American Buddhist nuns and as there was not anywhere Buddhist for them to go to they were going to Croagh Patrick instead. They were, they said, 'alms mendicants. We cannot have money at all, we can only eat between dawn and noon and the food must be given that day. It is an interesting and wonderful experience.' I gather that I made it rather more wonderful and interesting by buying them each a sausage roll, having first made sure that they were not vegetarians. These and one bread roll seemed to be their day's diet but they were remarkably cheerful, and I think it was at the prospect of food at last as they had not eaten that day. Of course I am now sorry that I did not also buy them three oranges and three croissants so they could have had a decent meal but I was in a great hurry to get some food down them before the clock struck twelve.

Clifden seemed a pleasant sort of place, perched high up above a little harbour at the bay of Ardbear. I was so taken up with the business of feeding nuns and getting my tape recorder fixed that I made no more interesting observations than that. I can, however, tell you that Clifden was called into being in 1812 by John D'Arcy Esquire who, according to the ever informative *Black's Guide* 'pointed out the advantages to the country which would arise from the establishment of a town in such a position. So late as the year 1815, Clifden had but one house, and now it has 400. It is unfortunate that the D'Arcys, who have done so much to raise the condition of this portion of Connemara, should have been reduced by their liberality. The representative of the family, the Rev. Hyacinth D'Arcy, is now incumbent of Omer, the parish of the town which his father founded, and the estate has passed from his hands. It was sold,' adds Murray sadly, 'under the Encumbered Estates Act.'

My nuns were planning to stop at Kylemore Abbey, which I also planned to visit, so I promised to report that they had been sighted and set off wondering whether three American Buddhist nuns are a more or a less remarkable find in mid Connemara than a covey of electricians capable of mending anything. At Kylemore Abbey I presented my dispatches to a girl called Fiona who was in charge of publicity. She said the Sisters were expecting to receive my nuns, as extending hospitality was part of the ethos of the Benedictine Order to which they belonged.

I was running short of words to describe, even to myself, the amazing beauty of the country through which I was passing, but Fiona produced a new word which was 'cradled', for she told me the magnificent mountains we could see were 'the Twelve Bens which cradle the coast of Connemara'.

Older writers call them the Twelve Pins, and to supplement my own inadequate powers of description I will tell you that Bartlett's *Scenery and Antiquities of Ireland* of 1841 says they are 'bare, but glittering with the aerial brilliancy peculiar to their formation. Their peaked summits rush together in elevations of 2,000 to 2,500 feet, a splendid cloud-pointing assemblage.'

Kylemore Abbey was built as a castle in the nineteenth century by a Manchester businessman called Mitchell Henry as a present for his Irish wife, on a spot by a lake where they had stopped to picnic on honeymoon. It cost him one-and-a-half million pounds so it was an expensive as well as an expansive gesture. I had noticed some years before that Scotland likewise had a lot of fairly new castles and wondered who had built them and why.

Fiona explained that it was to do with the poetry and novels of Walter Scott, whose romantic descriptions of the Scottish Highlands inspired Manchester businessmen and others to play at being chivalrous chieftains in remote Scottish fastnesses by building themselves castles and dressing in tartan. In building Kylemore Abbey in 1864, Mr Henry was following Queen Victoria and Prince Albert who were prime movers in this fashion, and started building at Balmoral in 1852.

Kylemore Castle was later bought by an American called Zimmerman as a wedding present for his daughter when she married the Duke of

138

Manchester, who lost it at cards, or at least had to part with it to pay his gambling debts. This all seemed a suitably romantic background to a very romantic spot but its later history was more sober.

It was acquired by Sisters of the Benedictine Order who arrived in Ireland from Ypres in 1916. The original Irish community was founded in Belgium at the time of the dissolution of the monasteries in the British Isles, and continued until the abbey in Ypres was destroyed by shelling in the 1914–18 War. Fourteen nuns of mixed nationality settled originally at Kylemore, which now accommodates an Abbess, 28 sisters, 85 school girls and a swarm of intelligent tourists who have had the good sense to come and see such a lovely spot.

From Kylemore I rode through an upland plain, cradled indeed by mountains, devoid of habitation and with peat workings or the occasional passing car as the only signs of human life. Then the road ran down for miles beside the sea loch that forms Killary Harbour, and into Leenane, on the borders of County Mayo.

So here I was, about a week into the expedition, with the feeling that rather a lot had happened, most of it satisfactory and much of it more than satisfactory. I thought at the time, and time has proved it true, that I would forever have the clearest recollection of the benevolent Willie Daley and of the man who told me about the Germans living in houseboats and of the nuns I had fed in Clifden. I can picture them all as I write, without the least difficulty. To some extent I had been going over ground that I had crossed before. Galway I had visited on the last trip, and I had just crossed into County Mayo to view the Aasleagh Falls, but otherwise what lay before me was altogether new.

MAYO

From Leenane I set off for Westport next day, taking the long way round on the far side of Killary Harbour and so into County Mayo. At the Aasleagh Falls I got some more news of the sea trout from a fisherman.

'Everywhere south of Achill the sea trout are consumed with the lice. The salmon farming is too big a thing for the government ever to stop it and that is the only thing that should be done.' I could not see why the lice affected the trout in the sea but not the salmon in the farms. He said it was because the salmon went further out to sea, to the Arctic, which killed the lice – but as the farmed salmon cannot do this it seemed a bit of a puzzle.

The road is signed to 'Delphi' and I knew that there was spot so named because some earlier Lord Sligo had been struck by the resemblance between it and the Delphi in Greece. I was therefore looking out to see if I could tell it for myself before being told I was there, and I could. The Greek Delphi has a cleft between two purplish rocks with the fountain of Castalia at the foot. In

Ireland there are two purplish rocks and the Boonderaga river below. The similarity would be greatly heightened if the bog at the bottom were planted with olive trees but as it is, it takes a bit of imagination and it was clever of Lord Sligo to spot it.

The books don't tell you which Lord Sligo made this ingenious observation, but I presume it was the second Marquis. He it was who in 1810 travelled in Greece for a time with the poet Lord Byron. 'Sligo,' wrote Byron, 'has a brig with fifty men who won't work, twelve guns that refuse to go off . . . he *would* travel with me to Corinth and has en suite a painter, a captain, a Gentleman misinterpreter (who boxes with the painter) besides sundry English varlets. We were obliged to have twenty nine horses in all.' Lord Sligo later got into trouble, apparently by enlisting some Royal Navy men onto his yacht. There was a row, wrote Byron, 'about his kidnapping the seamen. I, who know him, do not think him so culpable as the Navy are determined to make him.' I would like to find out more about this episode, but can only report that at the end of 1811 Byron wrote, in a good example of that figure of speech known as a zeugma, that 'Ld Sligo is in Ireland and a scrape.'

The road climbs up a valley with a few fine views over lakes as you look back. I paused to study a monument with this inscription:

DULOUGH PASS ROAD CONSTRUCTED BY THE CONGESTED DISTRICT BOARDS FOR IRELAND 1896

C. D. Oliver
Engineer

The creation of the Congested District Boards in 1890 was one of the measures taken up by A. J. Balfour as Chief Secretary for Ireland, to relieve the rural poverty of the west of the island, and to grapple with the existing Irish land system which he regarded as 'essentially and radically rotten'. The core of the problem lay in the hopelessly large number of hopelessly small agricultural holdings. Madame de Bovet in 1890 described the area of west Donegal, at which I would arrive later, like this:

> Do not go away with the idea that this wilderness is without inhabitants; on the contrary it is what is significantly called a 'congested district'. The parish of Gweedore, with its 68,000 acres, is divided among 1,777 little holders, who represent a population of 9,636 souls. The holdings vary from 5 to 10 acres; half of the ground is unproductive; the average rent is about one and sixpence an acre. It is much the same

as the adjoining districts – in short, in all the western littoral of the country, an area of 1,000 square miles, 100,000 human beings live on the very smallest amount that can sustain life, separated from the civilised world by an immense peat-moss and a double barrier of mountains.

The Congested Districts were to be found in the nine western counties from Donegal to Kerry. These districts had in them about half a million people who were divided, according to the Commissioners, into two classes; 'the poor, and the destitute'. Using money from the funds of the now-disestablished Protestant Church, the Boards built harbours, encouraged fisheries, built roads and railways, introduced cottage industries, and tried to improve agricultural methods. The Boards also bought up about two million acres of land which was redistributed in holdings of a reasonable size.

As I was leaning on my bicycle a car drew up and disgorged one of those extraordinary Frenchmen who go all round Ireland with hardly a word of English. He demanded to know the meaning of the monument before us, and I did my best to explain to him about the Congested District Boards, about which, I may say, I am rather better informed now than I was then.
He was so overjoyed to find that I could, in however halting a manner, converse in French that

he whipped out his map and insisted on telling me every detail of his holiday. Then when he found I was English he launched into a description of a visit he had made to some aeronautical establishment in England to test the effect of ice on the engines of Concorde. At least, I think that's what was going on – it was a very vivid description involving much crashing and banging and hiding behind walls but I am not altogether sure that I grasped the point exactly. I fancy that his trouble was that he had not spoken to anyone but his wife for a week and so was in urgent need of alternative conversation.

The road led on to a vast brown upland surrounded by mountain tips. It was boggy and had no sheep, no cows, no people, no telegraph wires, no houses. Eventually I came upon a man cutting turf (otherwise peat) or rather prodding it about with a rake, so I stopped to ask him about the turf-cutting process. He was rather more keen on telling me how it used to be done than how it is done now and I am sure that his explanation was perfectly clear but there was something wrong with my understanding as I could hardly make head or tail of it.

He spoke entirely in the present tense, which gave a graphic air to his description of a process which was now obsolete. 'You've a tool called a loy and one called a slane, an instrument for cutting turf with a little wing on it. You cut the bog two foot wide which is about twenty-four inches. The first thing you do is nick the straws, two straws each side, and then you come in with your loy and you throw it into the hollow bog. You place it evenly and you leave space for the water that is in the hollow bog to run away so that it doesn't lodge. You leave it in two neat lines and then you start with your slane and you nick your bank with your loy all the way along. Then you come back with your slane and you start cutting your turf. So you throw out the first spit about six foot and you go on like that for a hundred yards. Then the same way with the second spit, nick along the bank and throw it out, and you leave a space between the first spit of turf and the second line, the third line, and the fourth line, all the way along. The last spit is the best solid turf in the bog, we call it the hollow bog bit. You give it a week or a fortnight then you come back with your hands and you take the lines of turf and turn them the wet side up and the dry side down. In about another two weeks time you come along and foot the turf. You foot usually six sods or eight sods to it depending on the turf, and one on top, into little pockets, and that is a foot of turf.'

Nowadays a machine cuts a trench about four-and-a-half feet deep and eight inches wide and lays the contents out sideways, having separated the turf into long, thin parallel lines each eight inches wide. The process of drawing and footing seemed to be much the same, a foot of turf being a little cairn or pyramid through which the wind can blow to dry it. The turf is used 'twelve months of the year all round', he told me. I was aware of this, as in one place where I stayed an imp came staggering in through the dining room with a bucketful of turf 'for the range' in the kitchen.

This conversation reminded me that my father and his friend Rowntree had sparked off a strange rumour when on a walking tour of the west of Ireland in about 1912. Near Leenane they came upon a number of men cutting turf, and fell into conversation with them, much as I had done.

'Are you gentlemen from the Congested Board?' asked one of the turf cutters with an air of great suspicion.

'No,' they replied, 'we are just on a walking holiday.'

They went on, and two days later, in conversation at the pub where they were staying, they mentioned the turf cutting at Leenane.

'It has been stopped,' said the landlord.

'No,' said my father, 'it cannot have been stopped. We were there only two days ago, and they were doing it then.'

'Ah yes, but since then there has been two gentlemen from the Congested Board come along, and they have put a stop to it entirely.'

Why my father and his friend should have been taken for men from the Congested Board, or why the Board should be supposed to want to put a stop to turf cutting, are equally mysterious, but it shows the power of rumour in Ireland to fly ahead at greater speed than two young Englishmen on foot.

I thanked my own turf-cutting acquaintance, who was, I think, glad to pause from his not very strenuous labours and find someone new to talk to, which in so empty an area cannot happen very often. As I cycled off he was leaning on his rake in an attitude of contemplation, looking as if he were going over the old ways in his mind. I had enjoyed my conversation with him, mysterious as it was, and I warmed to his willingness to spend some time enlightening a complete stranger upon a subject of historical importance.

On I went, and in due course the great Croagh Patrick, Ireland's holy mountain, appeared on the right in the form of two towering peaks with lesser peaks between and beyond. The foothills are green, with purple above and grey at the summit. 'It was from this mountain,' said my ten-penny guidebook, 'that Saint Patrick banished snakes and toads from Ireland. Each time the Saint rang his bell he threw it over the precipice, accompanied by a swarm of venomous beasts. Every time angels brought the bell back to him until the process was completed.' This seems perhaps slightly at odds with a statement in the same guidebook that Saint Patrick drowned the last snake in Ireland in the Black Lough near Killarney, and is further contradicted by the beautiful ballad

'Saint Patrick was a Gentleman' which starts like this:

St Patrick was a gentleman, he came of decent
  people,
In Dublin town he built a church and on it put
  a steeple.
His father was a Callaghan, his mother was a
  Brady.
His aunt was an O'Shaughnessy and his uncle
  was a Grady.

Nine hundred thousand vipers blue he
  charmed with sweet discourses
And dined on them at Killaloo in soups and
  second courses.
The toads went hop the frogs went plop, slap-
  dash into the water
And all committed suicide to save themselves
  from slaughter.

I had found this in a book when looking up the
words of 'The Wearing of Green'. So, either at
Croagh Patrick, the Black Lough or Killaloo
(which I take to be the modern Killaloe) the
snakes were either eaten, drowned or went over a
precipice, and that is why there are none.

Although one might possibly be inclined to doubt
the authenticity of some of the foregoing, Saint
Patrick was certainly a historical figure. Some say
he came originally from Dunbarton in Scotland,

and others from Boulogne, but all agree that he was captured by slave traders and carried to Ireland, where he served six years as a herdsman. He then escaped to France, studied near Tours, and then at Auxerre, and returned as a missionary to Ireland in 432. To quote from W. A. O'Connor's *History of the Irish People*, Saint Patrick returned to Ireland 'fully instructed, formally authorised, and attended by numerous Irish Christians to plant the religion of the Cross from sea to sea. He not only made Ireland Christian, but he struck forth fountains of Christianity from every hill-side that have never ceased to flow.' Which observation, while poetical, seems from my observation to be entirely true.

I rode on, very happily indeed, through desolate moorland, passing through a village with the un-likely name of Louisburgh, to Westport, where I spent the night. It proved to be a disappointing town although the guidebook refers to it as 'a little bit of Latin Europe' and says 'the Mall is a wide avenue of limes with Georgian houses and a stream running down the centre, and the Octagon has been called the best designed public square in Ireland'. If this leads you to expect a sort of minor Bath, forget it. Ireland is like Greece, a land of sublime scenery and indifferent towns, and any town that is halfway decent is cried up beyond its merits from comparison with the rest. I fear this remark will cause resentment in Ireland, but for beautiful cities you had better go to France or Italy, and while we have plenty of terrible towns in England I never saw in Ireland anything to compare with Ludlow or Long Melford or some of the towns and villages of North Yorkshire, which is but to take these as examples at random.

There was a bookshop in Westport which stocked the £1 Penguin Classics and I bought *The Tenant of Wildfell Hall*. I have always disliked Penguins since their disgraceful behaviour in publishing *Lady Chatterley's Lover* and so releasing the tide of pornography which has overwhelmed every bookshop and bookstall in England though not, I am happy to say, in Ireland. The publishing of these cheap classics could be pleaded as a good deed in a naughty world, as they have made it possible to get something reasonable to read more or less anywhere, and at a price at which you can leave the book behind when you have finished it, so you need not carry it home. It is a pity that nobody bothers about accuracy though. It says on the cover of this edition of 'Wildfell Hall' that it is 'set in Regency times' but it isn't. The earliest episode is recorded in a diary entry dated 1 June 1821, at which date George IV was on the throne and not Prince Regent any longer.

After Westport and before Achill Island comes Newport, a smaller, less pretentious place than Westport with good houses beside the estuary and a fine main street. It is largely overlooked by

151

guidebooks in favour of Westport but I felt it would have been a better place to stay. I stopped for coffee that morning at a place run by the Sisters of Saint Lucy, and sat at a table next to two visiting American priests and one resident American sister. They were having a talking competition which the resident sister won without the least difficulty. The priests were reduced to the role of chorus and not allowed any independence of speech whatever. Once the sister had established the upper hand the talk went like this:

Sister: Father Guliani was the priest. He was the priest when I was there.
Priest: Father Guliani!
Sister: He used to teach the orphans. He always used to teach the orphans.
Priest: Orphans!
Sister: And as well he used to say mass in the prison every day. He came to the prison every day to say mass.
Priest: Oh golly!
Sister: Yes, every single day he used to say mass in the prison.
Priest: Oh my!

So it went on until the subject of travel came up, when one priest, in desperation, tried to tell a story about taking off from Shannon and running into a flock of birds, but the sister interrupted him smartly to say that she had been unable to land at Knock in a fog, was diverted to Dublin and carried back by bus.

Priest: Oh golly!

Between Newport and Achill Island you get a fine view of Clew Bay and a sea dotted with small islands. I turned aside to see a prehistoric gallery grave, which turned out to be a sort of hybrid between a dolmen and a wedge tomb, a big stone box with a top like a table. There was nobody there except a black cow which stared at me morosely. It was pleasant to think of the prehistoric men who built it and who must have given a terrific cheer when they got the top in place, as it is a huge flat slab of stone about six feet by eight, and eight inches thick, and must weigh many tons.

You cross to Achill Island by bridge, and once there it is all mountains, moorland, bogs and cliffs. I stayed with Mr and Mrs Gallagher and when I arrived Mrs Gallagher said to me, 'Where do you come from?' I made her guess and she said, 'France.' This surprised me as I thought I spoke better English than most French people. They had had a French couple staying the week before. 'They came for one night and stayed three and did concentrate mostly on fishing. The weather was suitable for them and they just caught one trout in two days but they were happy enough. They went to Donegal after that but how they got there the poor devils I don't know for they were seventy-one years each of them and spoke no English at all.'

I should think Mr and Mrs Gallagher were also 71 years each of them and they spent most of their time working in their superb vegetable garden, which quite altered my view of Irish peat bogs. There is bog all around their house, but their garden, which is nothing other than cultivated bog, grows a profusion of potatoes, carrots, cabbages, beans, lettuces, onions and shallots, and there is a glasshouse with tomatoes. I spent the next day cycling round Achill and I did not see another kitchen garden anywhere. I asked Mr Gallagher why no one else grew vegetables and he said, 'Too lazy. They'd rather buy from me.' It brought back to me a story which my father acquired on a visit to the Food and Agriculture Organisation in Rome. A young agricultural expert was talking to the headman of a South American village:

Expert: Does corn grow in this valley?
Headman: (sadly) No *señor*, no corn.
Expert: Or potatoes?
Headman: (more sadly) No *señor*, no potatoes.
Expert: Or tomatoes?
Headman: (even more sadly) No *señor*, no tomatoes.
Expert: Are you sure? Have you tried planting them?

Headman: Ah *señor*, if you plant them *of course* they grow.

Punch in its heyday used to have cartoons like that.

It seemed to me that most things would grow, though perhaps not always ripen, if planted in the bog at Achill, and if they wanted they could convert the whole island into a great market garden. But then again, perhaps they are right not to do so, because there are plenty of market gardens in the world but a diminishing number of unspoilt moorlands, and as Ireland is not short of food I am glad they prefer to leave Achill as it is.

I asked Mr Gallagher where I should go on my bicycle and he mentioned a castle which had belonged to Grace O'Malley, a lady whom the guidebooks call 'the famous pirate Queen'. Apart from a few odd anecdotes I had gathered very little about her so I asked Mr Gallagher to tell me more.

'She was a revolutionary woman, but I don't just remember much at all about her.'

'I believe she had an audience with Queen Elizabeth,' said I, hoping to jog his memory. 'They talked in Latin as that was the only language they had in common.'

'Would that be the mother of the present Queen Elizabeth?'

Now that was a fine picture, the Queen Mother smiling as ever while she was harangued in Latin by a female Irish pirate. Perhaps she could have interjected the odd '*Tempus Fugit*' or '*Domine Deus!*', and finally parted with a '*Vivat Regina*' dredged up from her memory of the coronation service.

I did not find the Grace O'Malley Castle but I went to Dugort where the Reverend Mr Nangle had, in 1834, embarked upon the hopeless project of converting the population to the Protestant religion. His church survives, a stern stone building in good repair, perched up high and overlooking a sandy beach. I paddled nearby in the Atlantic Ocean, sharing the beach with four cows, some hundred seagulls, and nobody else. The sun shone, the mountain of Slievemore towered above with its head just in the mist, and I wondered whether the Reverend gentleman had come on a fine day like this and thought, 'This is a kind of paradise. Perhaps if I make it a Protestant Paradise the idea will spread outwards.' He was a bit too optimistic. He achieved a certain success during the famine years, as charitable donations enabled him to feed the people of Achill and the prospect of starvation was a great aid to recruitment, but when the fear of death receded so did the people. I later met a doctor wandering around who seemed to know all about it and he said that at one time Mr Nangle had 182,000 children on his books to be fed, but it seems too many to be true. Outside his church there is a bell hung about six feet from the ground, so I rapped it with my knuckles and it rang surprisingly loudly. I tried to imagine 182,000 children coming to be fed at the sound of this bell, but the sheer emptiness of the site made it difficult. It was so entirely void and peaceful that to picture it as a well-organised refugee camp distributing food to lines of orderly children in such large numbers was beyond my imagination. Also I wondered about their parents, and whether they were quietly starving at home, but the knowledgeable doctor had disappeared so I could find out no more.

I find that it distresses those of my friends who like to pay extra for organic food when I point out that the great Irish potato famines of 1845–51 were a consequence of there being no alternative to organic farming. They take refuge in different forms of denial, such as trying to tell me that it was the fault of the Irish for cultivating a high-yielding potato with low resistance to potato blight, while there were sturdier but lower-yielding varieties around. For this I can find no evidence, and it was not the fault of the Irish in any way. Potato blight is a disease brought on by the fungus *phytophthera infestans*, which infects the leaves when the plant is growing. It can now be controlled by spraying but nobody knew this at the time. Had Irish farmers been able to spray their potatoes with that combination of copper sulphate and hydrated lime known

157

as Bordeaux mixture, or with copper sulphate and washing soda, which is called Burgundy mixture, these two being early basic fungicides, they would not have done themselves any harm and the crop could have been saved. As it was, when the blight struck the potatoes rotted.

In August 1846, a Father Mathew described what was a common scene: 'On the 27th of last month I passed from Cork to Dublin, and this doomed plant bloomed in all the luxuriance of an abundant harvest. Returning on the 3rd instant, I beheld with sorrow one wide waste of putrefying vegetation. In many places the wretched people were seated on the fences of their decaying gardens, wringing their hands, and wailing bitterly at the destruction that left them foodless.'

Ireland in the 1840s had a population of over eight million, of whom about half depended on the potato for food. It is possible to criticise the English government for not doing more by way of relief, and many people do, but famine on this scale can easily overwhelm the available resources even today. As it was, in 1845 Sir Robert Peel, on his own responsibility, arranged for the government to buy and distribute £100,000 worth of Indian corn from the United States. The generally hostile *Freeman's Journal* said in 1847 that 'No man died of famine during his administration, and it is a boast of which he might well be proud.' Peel went out of office in 1846, and thereafter the government's relief efforts were less effective, largely due to their regarding the problem as an Irish one to be solved within Ireland itself. In spite of this, by August 1847 over three million people were being fed at public expense. The voluntary efforts by individuals like Mr Nangle, by societies and committees, and particularly by the Society of Friends, had by then been overtaken by the scale of the disaster. It is reckoned that between 1845 and 1850 about one million people died of hunger or disease as a result of the potato famine.

E. C. Large, in his brilliant book *The Advance of the Fungi*, quotes from *The Times* of 1845 a typical annual budget for a small tenant with six months' casual labour:

	£	s	d
Wages	3.	18	0
Value of Pig	4	0	0
	7	18	0
Deduct Rent	5	0	0
Balance	2	18	0

On this, Large comments: '£2.18.0 per annum, to buy meal, clothing, tools, candles, medicine, drink, and every other luxury or necessity for a human family. While the middlemen and the landowners took the man's pig and a quarter of his wages, it was not difficult to perceive that without the potatoes the family would starve.'

The blight became endemic in Ireland, with

outbreaks of varying severity from year to year according to the weather, as damp conditions favour the fungus. It was not until the 1890s that the value of spraying with Bordeaux mixture was established by scientific experiment. It then took time to develop machinery and persuade potato farmers, in the words of E. C. Large 'to take up arms against the fungi and engage in chemical warfare with *phytophthera infestans*'. The practice of potato spraying only became universal in Ireland during the 1914–18 War, when it was given a boost as a measure to safeguard food supplies.

While riding back from Mr Nangle's church at Dugort I fell in with a man who was driving two cows with lively calves along the road, and as the calves kept going off at tangents into the bog I gave him a hand. I asked if he had any more animals and he said he hadn't. He cut winter feed for these cows and he had a piece of bog where he cut turf and that was what he did. There were a few sheep running around but not an enormous number, and in general on Achill Island there is very little sign of anybody doing anything much at all. The effect is to make it very peaceful as well as beautiful.

Next day I set off for Bangor. The Frenchman to whom I had spoken on the Dulough Pass Road got frightfully excited about the road from Mulrany, outside Achill, to Bangor. 'C'est un désert,' he kept saying, stabbing excitedly at the map with his finger. As far as Ballycroy it was quite a well-populated desert with a house every now and then and three places where I could, and one where I did, buy my lunch. Then Mayo became like no other county that I had seen in Ireland. The stone walls disappeared and were replaced by wire fences. Some of the fields were of forty or fifty acres instead of the usual little ones and there were farms with Dutch barns nestling under a range of rolling green hills. Clearly in these parts the soil is indeed capable of producing anything at all. If one thought some cosmic cataclysm was impending, which is quite a reasonable thing to think, it would be a sensible move to settle here with a good supply of seeds and garden tools.

Outside Ballycroy (and I never seemed to get inside Ballycroy, so either it does not exist as a village or I passed through without noticing) I talked to a man piling up turf. 'It's a brilliant heat. And inside our house now as well as the range we've an open fire from olden times and we kept it. It's beautiful on a winter's night if you're at a roasting fire.' He was, he said, 'a small farmer – sheep and a few cattle, with eighty acres and sixty more in commonage with another person. The like of us around here are just ticking over, nothing to spare but we don't mind. Once you're able to get along reasonably and be happy, that's the main thing.'

He most hospitably asked me in for a cup of tea, to which his wife added a pile of tomato sandwiches. He had been a bit of an actor in his time, having taken part in a television production called *The Ballroom of Romance*. 'The title I had in it was the Man with the Long Arms. My arms were not that long but I was supposed to be a hill farmer and lifting stones and building fences was supposed to have my arms made long. I'd to walk around and dance with the girls and I was in it nearly every day.'

In the house of the Man with the Long Arms I made a terrible mistake. His wife said that she had been campaigning for a regional technical college in Mayo, as at present the young people had to go to Galway. The words I used were these: 'I don't want to be impolite about any of your country, but I didn't really like Galway. There are too many skinheads and drop-outs and young people with rings in their noses and I don't think I would like my children to have to live there.' Now an Irishman could speak in such terms of London or Bristol or Bath and no one would mind at all but beware of saying such things in Ireland if you are an Englishman. Be warned by me that the correct view is that Galway is a superior city to Florence, Venice is nothing compared to it, and the skinheads are the most delightful people once you get to know them. I had to grovel my way out of the house protesting that I would return to Galway with an open mind and would certainly endeavour to cultivate the acquaintance of the skinheads, feeling meanwhile that I had abused the Long-armed Man's hospitality most dreadfully.

★   ★   ★

After Ballycroy the desert came into its own. I could see for 20 miles in every direction without a human habitation in view, and at Bangor Erris, where I stayed, I looked from my room across miles of empty bog to Slievemore.

I liked Mayo extremely much. Although it is just as beautiful as Galway or Connemara, it seems to have had less publicity and so far fewer tourists. It was therefore a bit of a surprise to find at Brogan's grocery in Bangor a sign saying:

Welcome
Willkommen
Bienvenue

as it felt as if Bangor was a place that I had found by myself as an act of original discovery. Perhaps the *Willkommens* and *Bienvenues* come for the fishing as the pub owner told me that the sea trout were present in thousands, there being no salmon farming in these parts, thus confirming that for sea trout you must go north of Achill. The same pub owner gave me a pint of Guinness; salmon steak, chips and vegetables; apple pie and coffee, for £7.65, thus further confirming my impression that food in Ireland had taken a turn for the very much better since my earlier trip.

Next day I took a small road through more desert, enjoying Ireland at its best, shedding clothing along the way and putting on a sunhat. This had been used before but only for the ridiculous purpose for keeping in place the hood attached to my waterproof. This hood if left to itself either blew back and did no good at all but simply filled with water, or else blew forward and obscured my eyes so that I could not see where I was going. I found that if I put the sunhat on top and fixed the chinstrap under my chin the whole contraption stayed in place and kept the rain off at the cost of looking silly. Now for the first time I needed the sunhat without the hood, in its own right to keep the sun off. The road was pretty level, my enemy the West Wind was absent, the countryside was utterly beautiful and latterly the Atlantic took to trying to pretend it was the Mediterranean by being bright blue and benevolent looking. If Ireland were always like this everyone would want to live there and the place would be utterly ruined.

Somewhere along the way there was a pub where I stopped for coffee. The entire Republic at this time was obsessed with the World Cup, for which Ireland had qualified and which was soon to start. The Minister of Justice, a woman, had annoyed the publicans by refusing to grant an extension of opening hours on World Cup nights, so denying the male part of the population the right to get properly drunk in celebration or lamentation as the case might require. The television was on in the pub, as it always was throughout the whole country, and after a few minutes Jackie Charlton appeared, as he always did whenever the television was on anywhere. If he wasn't talking about football he was talking about something else and I got to know quite a lot about him, such as that he is very keen on Weetabix, finds his Access card very useful, drinks a lot of milk, and is impressed by the service he gets from some Irish bank or other. As soon as he appeared all conversation stopped while we listened to what he had to say. This time, as I drank my coffee, there were a few shots of Irish players practising, and then it was explained that while they were all whinging about the heat, this was part of Jack's master plan. He got them over early to wherever it was so that they had eight days in which to whinge, and after that they would get bored with whinging and start playing proper football.

After that I turned in to visit an archaeological site called 'the Céide Fields', but the way they pronounced it sounded like 'the KGB' as Céide seems to be pronounced 'Cagey', more or less. However you pronounce them, they make up a revealing piece of archaeology which has laid bare from under the bog a neolithic farming civilisation that precedes the pyramids by five hundred years, or otherwise dating from about 3000 BC. They have uncovered walls, houses, implements and pottery, and worked out the system of agriculture and concluded that it was a vast settlement extending over four square miles, of a very peaceful nature as there were no signs of fortifications or

165

any defensive arrangements. It is quite a recent excavation which has, they say, altered many earlier views of Stone-Age civilisation. Although there is now bog all around it seems that such settlements were once to be found throughout North Mayo, making it a well-populated area at the time.

From the Céide Fields the road took me via Killala where there is a round tower inferior to that at Killmacduagh as it has no scuff marks from boots. The French General Humbert landed at Killala in 1798 with just over one thousand men to make a brief attempt at stirring up rebellion. He succeeded in defeating the local militia, who ran off so quickly that the battle is known as the Castlebar Races. They think well of General Humbert at Killala in consequence, and have named a school after him and put up a bust of him on the way out of town.

From there I went to Ballina where I made a surprising discovery. Not far from my B&B was a sign to Belleek Castle Hotel. I asked my landlady if I could get a meal there, and she said it was only ten minutes ride away so I had better go and find out, for she did not know herself. I cycled up through a sort of park with beech trees and rang the bell of what looked like a grey stone Elizabethan manor house. The massive studded doors swung open and the first impression was of wood, beautiful wood. In the middle of the hall was a carved refectory table of that sort of oak that you have to stroke because you cannot help it. I was fondling refectory tables and carved fireplaces while admiring the bronzes and the tapestry behind the receptionist, rejoicing in the feel of it all, when the owner arrived and took me through into the Armada bar, which was even better. I knew that the Spanish Armada had foundered at different points along the coast of Ireland in 1588, but I was not prepared for relics of it to be found at places like the Belleek Castle Hotel. The bar itself was made of a huge timber baulk recovered from an Armada galleon by a means which the owner did not care to discuss. He had trimmed it by hand with an adze to get off all the rotten bits and then polished it. The room has more timber from Armada galleons, and the building and furnishings are altogether magnificent, with such features as self-supporting staircases seemingly hanging in air, tapestries, and beautiful panelling. There is also a dungeon with a sinister creaking door, which houses a collection of helmets and shields and swords and battleaxes and lances and other items of a medieval nature, all of which make up an armoury which would do credit to the Tower of London or Windsor Castle. Then there is a figurehead from a Spanish galleon in the form of a woodworm-riddled and very handsome old gentleman who was broken off at the knees and looks like a battered Don Quixote. The beamed roof of the medieval banqueting hall is supported by stone columns with fine carved capitals. In the old kitchen is a hen-coop/dresser with ordinary shelves above but slatted compartments below, from which the heads of stuffed chickens protrude. Live chickens would once have spent the night there, 'at a point of time', to starve preparatory to being eaten next day.

The owner declared the pièce de résistance to be a room full of fossils with an ichthyosaurus on the wall, a mammoth's tooth or two, ammonites galore, and I know not what else. I could see that it was a fossil collector's paradise if you are into fossils, which I am not, but I was more impressed by Grace O'Malley's bed, a beautifully carved oak four-poster recovered from Clare Island. It was obviously Grace O'Malley's bed because she lived on Clare Island and nobody below the rank of queen would have such a magnificent bed. Just for good measure, the last wolf in Ireland, killed at Maam Cross in 1712, stands in a passage, stuffed. As a sort of throwaway line they told me that the first Irish horse to win the Grand National was foaled here, his name being Bonny Prince Charlie.

There was really no end to the excitement, not by any means excluding the dinner which I ate by candlelight in baronial splendour, and concluded that the cook was a genius. The meal consisted of garlic mushrooms; (excellent!) fish chowder; pork medallions; profiteroles; coffee; two pints of Guinness and it was all delicious including the home-baked bread rolls which I kept eating and so ate far too much. It came to £21.50 which I thought was a pretty good steal, and I cycled away marvelling at having made such a remarkable discovery in a fairly remote part of County Mayo. My hot tip for anyone anywhere near Ballina is 'Don't miss the Belleek Castle Hotel.' I cannot work the Internet, but my daughter can, and she tells me that its details are to be found there.

More to be expected in Ballina than the treasures I have just described was the venerable horse-dealer Mr Joe Sweeney. I sought him out on the advice of the owners of Belleek Castle, who told me he was a man I ought to talk to. I got directions to his house, walked through a small farmyard, knocked at the door and explained that I was cycling through Ireland with a tape recorder and would like to speak to Mr Sweeney for the benefit of the BBC. The lady who opened the door showed no surprise but showed me in to Mr Sweeney at once. He proved to be a small old man sunk in the depths of an armchair, in which he stayed fixed, with a cup of tea balanced on the arm, which he did not drink. He talked to me very readily on the subject of horse-dealing.

He was, he said, 'a poor sort of farmer but a horse-dealer all my life. To tell you about horse-dealing, you would never learn it, no matter who he is. You could see a horse all right today and when you'd buy him and have him a while there could be something wrong with him. It's very hard to be a judge and we have very bad vets.' ('Vets' being pronounced 'vits' and spoken with venom. I should explain, for those who do not go in for horses, that it is standard practice when buying a horse to make an offer 'subject to the vet'. This means that the buyer will get a veterinary surgeon to examine the horse, and if he passes it fit and sound, the bargain is concluded, but if he turns it down, the deal is off.)

'Both in Ireland and England the vits turn a horse down for anything. It shouldn't be. There's not many good vits that we have – the vit reads it out of a book, but we started the hard way. The time I started, it was walking them from fair to fair, there was no such thing as lorries. You'd to ride them, maybe five or six or seven altogether tied up, it could be fifty miles or sixty miles or seventy miles. I've rode horses from Galway to here.'

I remember a painting by Sir Alfred Mannings called *The Ford* which shows a man in a cloth cap riding one horse and leading two others, one in each hand, with two or three more tagging along behind. The whole lot are splashing through a river, and the picture could be Mr Sweeney to the life.

The standard of honesty had fallen a lot he said.

'We get it very hard to do now. It's what the world is going mad for money. You'd see a feller come in a big flashy car with him and all that, and give me a cheque in and you'd have to be waiting and hold the horses until you see whether the money come up. Since I started in the horse business I've seen a great many coming and going. There's people as went into it and what brought them into it is – they have the wealth. They wouldn't have started as poor as I did. In the old days it was ten pounds, five pounds, twenty pounds for a horse. It could be a great horse for them prices, but then it came into thousands. Ah, there's different times, there's different times!'

On my very first visit to Ireland, when I was 17, I spent some time in the company of a horse-dealer called Tommy Grantham, who had arrived from England and was also staying with my friends. He let me come with him to a horse fair, I think at Clonmel, where he bought several animals. There was no bother with vits. Tommy looked in each horse's eyes and mouth, ran his hand down each leg, got the owner to trot it up and down, and if in any doubt about its merits, got on and cantered it about himself. If he didn't like it he shook his head, and if he did like it the bargaining began. If successful, this ended in the owner spitting on his hand and offering it to Tommy to shake, which he stoutly did. Tommy's stables in England were close to where we lived, and I knew that when I got back all the horsey people would be agog to know how much Tommy paid when buying horses, to compare with what he charged when selling them. Thinking this to be privileged information which I was better off without, I always moved out of earshot when they began to haggle over the price.

Tommy Grantham did not gather his purchases into a string and ride off at the head of them like Mr Sweeney, he just wrote cheques and got in his car and rode off in that. He was well known in those parts and there was some method whereby his horses were collected up and shipped to England. This, and the fact that no one ever thought his cheques would bounce, were the only differences between his system and Mr Sweeney's.

Ballina is close to the border between Mayo and Sligo. Having thanked Mr Sweeney for his kindness in talking to me, I got on my bicycle and crossed that border, taking the coast road to Sligo. I was in a very happy state, with plenty to muse upon as I rode along, especially the treasures and delights of the Belleek Castle Hotel, and the ways of horse-dealers past and present.

SLIGO AND DONEGAL

Shortly after crossing the border I went wrong for the first time on this trip. The map showed a main road going straight to Sligo, but I thought it best to avoid this in favour of a minor road marked R297. It is so marked on the map, but the R297 is not marked as anything at all on the ground, and whatever road I was on had a decided tendency to fork and branch off into other roads of equal size with itself but without any indication of where any of them were going. It was quite pleasant, because I got a good view out to sea over Killala Bay, and it was interesting because the farms were much bigger and often looked quite English. I saw 60 Friesian cows in a field and there was silage in big bags and hay in big bales which needed a tractor to lift them, all of which was a far cry from the little bales, and even haycocks, which I had seen back in Connemara.

Evidently Sligo has always been something like this, or at least it was in 1890 when Madame de Bovet went before me on the road from Ballina to Sligo. 'The physiognomy of the country changes,' she says. 'Less bog, better kept farms, good crops of barley, oats and rye, great fields of beetroot instead of the everlasting potato, more numerous and fatter cattle – these are the signs of prosperity. The children go barefoot, but that is a fixed custom in Ireland, and they seem none the worse for it. The country has become more tame, but that is rather a relief, for one wearies of rugged grandeur. There remains a softened and peaceful beauty which rejoices the eye without putting a strain upon the faculty of admiration.'

I perfectly agree with what Madame de Bovet says, with two exceptions. I saw no fields of beetroot and when, by bearing generally eastward, I found my way onto the R297 to Ballysadare, the children in my B&B were wearing shoes.

It was here that I realised that whoever is Secretary of State for Education in England should study the system of education in Ireland, where standards are known to be high and the secret is obviously Boundless Competition and Unceasing Bribery. All the houses where there are children are crammed with trophies and medallions which have been won for passing exams, Gaelic dancing, football, the hundred yards and almost anything else which can be made a competition of. The exams for the Leaving Certificate, commonly called the Leaving, were in progress and provided the second general topic of conversation throughout the country, after the World Cup. It was agreed on all sides that the Gaelic paper had been unreasonably hard, but

I had read in a newspaper that the French Comprehension was 'student friendly', which I supposed to mean easy, so I was able to contribute this as my part of any discussion. The Leaving provokes the same rash of ominous-looking Good Luck cards as A Levels in England and causes the same air of brooding anxiety to pervade the house, all of which were evident where I stayed in Ballysadare.

The next day I paused at Carrowmore, just before Sligo itself, where there is a great megalithic cemetery with cairns, sepulchral chambers, dolmens and stone circles all grouped together. It seemed to be a community of the dead, unlike the Céide Fields which was a community of the living. The explanation given is that at Céide Fields they had a settled agricultural way of life with permanent houses and fields, whereas around Sligo they existed by hunting and fishing, and lived in wigwams in a forest, so their only lasting memorial was their burial ground. One of the excavated graves could almost be called cosy. It was a comfortable little underground room with a single stone on top, some nine feet by twelve in size and the roof a foot thick. There were neatly-mown paths all about the cemetery and you stroll from one thing to the next with the Ox Mountains, Ben Bulben and the King's Mountain forming a natural stone circle all around. It is like a superior form of golf – a delightful walk in wonderful surroundings but without the aggravation of chasing a little white ball. The people at the ticket office looked at my recording machine, which was in the process of going wrong again, and called it 'prehistoric', a word which obviously rose to their lips because of the surroundings.

The sun was shining, and I was in cycling mode, so I pressed on through the town of Sligo without stopping. This must have been a mistake as there is an abbey and an art gallery which I ought to have seen. The gallery has paintings, I now realise, by Jack Yeats the painter, who I prefer to W. B. Yeats, his brother the poet. One of my difficulties with the poet is that I do not believe that he ever meant to live in a clay and wattle cabin on a diet of beans and honey.

> I will arise and go now, and go to Innisfree,
> And a small cabin build there, of clay and
> wattles made:
> Nine bean rows will I have there, a hive for
> the honey bee
> And live alone in the bee-loud glade.

If he didn't mean to do it he had no business to say that he did, but perhaps I am too literal-minded and the poem is really symbolic and about death, or some other serious subject.

Beyond Sligo you come to Drumcliff, where Yeats was buried and which is the only place north of County Galway where I found tourists in any quantity. Germans are evidently enthusiastic Yeats-lovers, because Greimann Reisen and Co. were delivering them in abundance to look at his grave. The inscription on it is: 'Cast a cold eye on life, on death. Horsemen, pass by.' The German party regarded it solemnly for a decent time, then climbed back into their bus and passed by.

As well as Yeat's gravestone there is a fine High Cross of great antiquity coming from the eleventh century or thereabouts. It is carved with Daniel in the Lions' Den, Adam and Eve, Cain killing Abel and Christ in Glory. Or so they said. They were simple little carvings and could have been anything as far as I could tell.

Near Drumcliff a brawl or set-to, known as the Battle of the Books, took place between Saints Columba and Finian. Saint Columba borrowed a psalter from Saint Finian and made a copy of it. Saint Finian claimed the copyright and demanded the copy, which Saint Columba refused to give him. King Dermot ruled in Saint Finian's favour, declaring 'the calf goes with the cow'. Saint Columba would not abide by his decision and the two sides came to blows in a most unsaintly manner, Saint Columba winning. In a fit of remorse he later retired to Iona to convert the Scots, so some good came of it at last.

I turned off on a deviation to look at Lissadell House, home of the Gore-Booth family. It was built in 1833 for Sir Robert Gore-Booth and passed to his son Sir Henry William Gore-Booth, who the *Dictionary of National Biography* describes as a 'philanthropist and explorer'. W. B. Yeats was a regular visitor, hence his poem to Sir Henry's two daughters 'In memory of Eva Gore-Booth and Con Markievicz'. It starts:

> The light of evening, Lissadell,
> Great windows open to the south,
> Two girls in silk kimonos, both
> Beautiful, one a gazelle.

As well as beautiful they were both suffragettes, Constance the more colourful. They had unlikely careers for girls who had been educated by governesses and brought up to hunt and shoot in Ireland. Constance persuaded her parents to let her enrol at the Slade School of Art in London where she met and married a Polish widower, Count Casimir Dunin-Markievicz. This, you would think, must have caused some alarm at Lissadell, with more to follow when she gave up art for politics and became a passionate supporter of the armed struggle against England. She took part in the Easter Rising of 1916, for which she was sentenced to death, later commuted to life imprisonment, and she served 14 months of the sentence until she was released in the general amnesty of 1917. It is a little difficult to keep track of her subsequent arrests and imprisonments but she certainly did two spells of hard labour and mounted a hunger strike. From prison in 1918 she became the first woman to be elected to the British Parliament, having stood successfully as a Sinn Féin candidate, but, like all Sinn Féin members so far, did not take her seat. The Yeats poem was written in 1927, the year in which she died, and Yeats speaks of her later political career in melancholy terms:

> The older is condemned to death,
> Pardoned, drags out lonely years
> Conspiring among the ignorant.

I found that this note of melancholy was echoed at Lissadell House itself, where overgrown trees blocked the view from the front and where the wallpaper was peeling off in the damp inside. The heads of dead deer, trophies perhaps of the philanthropic explorer, were mounted on the walls, thick with dust and eaten with moth. The guide made the best of it, assuring his audience that all is in its original untouched state, but it would have been better if they had touched it up a bit, at least to the extent of dusting the deer now and again.

The whole place reminded me of Lord Scamperdale's great house in the novel *Mr Sponge's Sporting Tour*, written by the Victorian sporting novelist R. S. Surtees. Called Woodmansterne, Lord Scamperdale's house had come down through several generations to the current Earl 'according to the usual alternating course of great English families – one generation living and the next starving'. The fourth Earl, says Surtees 'was a man of *vertù* – a great traveller and collector of coins, pictures, statues, marbles and curiosities generally – things that are very dear to buy but oftentimes extremely cheap when sold; and, having collected a vast quantity from all parts of the world (no easy feat in those days) he made them heirlooms and departed this life, leaving the next earl the pleasure of contemplating them. The fifth earl having duly starved through life, then made way for the sixth; who, finding such a quantity of valuables stowed away as he thought, in rather a confined way, sent to London for a first-rate architect, Sir Thomas Squareall (who always posted with four horses), who forthwith pulled down the old brick-and-stone Elizabethan mansion, and built the present splendid Italian structure of the finest polished stone at an expense of, – furniture and all – say, one hundred and twenty thousand pounds, Sir Thomas's estimate being thirty thousand pounds.'

Lissadell House was seemingly built on a similar principle, probably by a pupil of Sir Thomas Squareall and stocked by a liver who was a man of *vertù*. The present generation of owners give the impression of being starvers. There was no sign of them in the main rooms and they have made themselves, according to the guide, a habitable corner somewhere into which I expect, like Lord Scamperdale, they 'creep quietly by a side door opening from the outer entrance and so save frequent exposure to the cold and damp of the large cathedral-like hall beyond'.

The otherwise dispiriting tour of the house was enlivened by a bright and attractive American girl with lovely eyes. There was a piano in the music room and this she whipped open and then boldly struck a few chords, causing it to give out dust and a jarring noise. 'That was a spirited attack on the piano,' I said, which broke the ice and enabled us to chat unobtrusively while the guide went prosing on. There was some Greek-looking china on a table about which I said, 'It looks like tourist trash which some dead Gore-Booth brought back from Corfu.'

'Could be,' she said.

'Let's pick some up and have a look. Better stand between me and the guide.' So she did, and we examined a couple of bits together. They proved to be much heavier than expected. 'Old tourist trash,' she decided.

'There will be a clatter when I put them back, so you have got to create a diversion,' whereupon she broke into a paroxysm of coughing which effectively drowned all other noise.

As well as beautiful eyes she had lovely manners and thanked the guide in the most delightful way for making it all so interesting, although it was not. She herself was a good deal more interesting than anything else in the house, and of this she was, of course, aware. In talking to me she occasionally laid her hand on my arm, obviously thinking, 'Might as well bewitch this old fellow just for practice.' Still, I felt I could have been in with a chance if certain obstacles had been removed, such as 40 years from my age, and the dour and brooding young man with a close-cropped head by whom she was accompanied.

That night I spent on a point by the sea at Streedagh in a house which I found by accident. There was a sign on the main road advertising 'Mount Edward Lodge', which sounded just the place for me, so I turned off in search of it but before I reached it I was diverted by another sign which said 'Fresh Sea Food.' The house belonged to a fisherman so the seafood was as fresh as could be. The main course that night was salmon and prawns, plus organic rice with garlic butter, a combination I had not come across before and which I heartily recommend.

I had for company, so far as they were any company, a party of Italians who arrived on horseback at a quarter past nine at night. They took their horses into a field which I could see from my window. The time taken for seven Italians to take seven horses into a field, remove their saddles and bridles and give each of them a bucket of food, is 36 minutes by my watch. They were chattering wildly in Italian all the while, the word *mangiare* coming into it a lot, but whether they meant *mangiare* for themselves or the horses I could not make out. They made rather a mess of the *mangiare* business as far as the horses went, as the animals kept stealing each other's food and kicking each other's ribs. The system for riding tours was, I discovered, to hand the tourists some horses and a map and let them get on with it. This seemed a very trusting approach, especially as they were pretty good horses, but the riders only ride on the beaches or the small roads and so they do not get lost or bolted with very often.

At Streedagh there is a plaque and a full-sized model of the bow of a ship to commemorate the three Armada vessels which foundered there. The plaque has a map showing where the other 18 went down, strung out along the west and north coasts of Ireland. I talked to my fisherman host about what went wrong at Streedagh, and as a man of the sea he understood it exactly. 'There's here the remains of three ships, the *Juliana*, the *Lavia*, and the *Santa Maria*. They were wrecked on the beach for they took shelter in sou-westerly gales and the wind went round to nor-west. They could not help being wrecked for they were doing the right thing alright if the wind didn't change, but it did.'

The Irish, who had no reason to love Queen Elizabeth, nevertheless with exemplary loyalty generally hanged or cut the throats of those Armada Spaniards who got ashore. At Streedagh though they were mostly drowned, to the number of eleven hundred. From Streedagh I set off for Donegal crossing the narrow neck of County Leitrim which connects the rest of that county to the sea. There is a miniature Stonehenge at a place called Creevykeel. This struck me as a wonderful Dickensian name, and I pictured Mr and Mrs Creevykeel in genteel poverty with far too many children amid scenes like this:

'Mr Creevykeel, my dear.'
'Yes, my life?'
'Your sleeve is in the marmalade, my own.'
'So it is, my love,' said Mr Creevykeel, and absent-mindedly wiped his cuff on the head of Benjamin, who was so named in the unsuccessful hope that he would be the last born.

The Creevykeel of fact rather than of my imagination is a wedge-shaped mound with a burial chamber off the central court and two further passage graves. It is far bigger and better than anything I had seen in the Burren and I shared it briefly with a man from Lichfield who took my photograph, and I took his. Then he left and I had it to myself, with any prehistoric ghosts that may happen to haunt it.

About this time I realised I had become a connoisseur of road surfaces. This is not a matter of potholes, in which respect the Irish roads are generally pretty good, but of the finish which is given to the road by the engineer who builds it. Nice, kind engineers make roads with a glassy black surface of the sort that melts in the sun, as this is ideal for cycling and a bicycle bowls along marvellously. Next after that come small stones fitted closely together, and last of all and by far the worst are the roads made by engineers who put down wet tar and scatter small stones loosely on top. This produces an effect like a badly-made mosaic with gaps between the stones, and as soon as you get onto that surface you feel the bicycle check. It is like having a heavy tread on your tyres, only in this case the tread is actually on the road, so the road grips the bicycle and the bicycle grips the road and almost stops. If all road engineers were really benevolent they would either use the smoothest of tarmac all the time or they would at least make cycle tracks of it at the side. I have a high opinion of the County Engineer of County Donegal because, although he uses the bad-mosaic method in the middle, he generally seems to provide, at least by the main roads, a glassy hard shoulder for the benefit of cyclists. From Streedagh to Donegal town I was blown along by a south-west wind on an admirable road surface in a state of high exultation.

Donegal town was said by my guidebook to be 'a trim and quiet little place at the mouth of the

River Eske'. The only entry I made in my note-book was 'wandered around Donegal, not much impressed' so perhaps that is really all there is to be said for it. Next day I did my best to make up for my lack of tourist enterprise in Donegal by climbing up a very steep hill to Mountcharles, a village which claims to have one of the finest eighteenth-century houses in Ireland. Very likely it has, but as there are no signs to tell you where it is I was down the other side of the hill by the time I realised I had missed it. I came to a bridge at Eeny Water, where the fishing was only ten pounds per day according to the sign, and the catch limited to three fish. A farmer called James assured me that it was very good fishing, and it is a very lovely river, so I mention the matter in case it is useful information for any keen fish-ermen who may read this book.

The road from there to Ardara goes through a wild upland and arrives at Portnoo, where I would have been glad to stop had there been anywhere that did not overlook a caravan site, so I went on to Dungloe. The road at first is of the sort most annoying to cyclists because it goes down for the sake of going up, and up for the sake of going down. Then it emerges onto the rather sinister and inhospitable area called The Rosses, which consists of miles and miles of empty moorland with little lakes and outcrops of granite here and there. I went for 15 miles without a bed-and-breakfast sign, and at about four o'clock a mist came down, at which I began to entertain the eerie thought that I might possibly be benighted on the moor with a puncture or some other breakdown. I wasn't though, and got to Dungloe all right, where, as I entered the pub where I stayed that night a man looked up from his beer, noticed me, and said, 'Jesus, it's Bobby Charlton!' I do rather resemble that hero and if I could have simulated a Geordie accent well enough for the error to be persisted in, it would have given me a kind of second-hand sainthood as his brother Saint Jack had just about displaced Saint Patrick in the Irish calendar as a result of his enormously successful management of the Irish football team.

I found next day, after a ride across some more Rosses, that this part of Donegal is so determinedly Gaelic that they have abandoned the use of English on their signposts altogether. I had meant to make it a short ride ending at Gweedore but it turned into an even shorter one because of this difficulty. When I reached Loughanure, I found that the place from which I had just come and which yesterday had been called Dungloe, had now been turned into An Clochan Liath. The only place named in the direction in which I was going was called Croicsli, so I assumed that what was Croicsli today was what yesterday had been known as Gweedore, and so there I stopped. This was a foolish mistake, and I should have known that Gweedore was today called Gaoth Doshair and was five miles further on from where I was. But I do not repine, as the house where I stayed in Croicsli was a lovely place run by lovely people.

I did my own washing for once and hung it on the line, then went for a walk and was out for three hours among hills, lakes and rocks. There was a long thin waterfall at one point, some sheep now and again, but no people. When I got back they had spread my washing on radiators all round the house and lit a blazing turf fire in the parlour (I am sure it was a parlour and not a lounge) which they insisted on giving up to me and sitting in the kitchen themselves. They had asked when I arrived if I wanted a cup of tea and it came with a pile of ham sandwiches and was my lunch. That night it was terribly wet and as I was girding myself to go out in search of a meal they knocked on the door: 'We have some dinner for ourselves – would you like some?' So I sat by my turf fire in the parlour and ate a plateful of steak, potatoes and vegetables, with a glass of milk, followed by bread and butter and tea. I had the usual noble breakfast next morning and when I came to settle up, 'That will be twelve pound,' they said.

'You cannot have twelve pounds,' said I, 'you have given me three meals so you must have twenty pounds, though that is not really enough.'

'What three meals?' asked my hostess.

'A pile of ham sandwiches and tea; an excellent dinner; and breakfast.'

'What is a cup of tea? It is nothing at all,' she

said, blithely ignoring sandwiches worth three pounds at a modest computation. 'I will not take twenty pounds.'

So we battled on and at last I beat the bill up to £15 but that was the best I could do, and a hard struggle it was.

My host was, he said, a small farmer with 80 mountain ewes. 'We have a quarter of a thousand acres of commonage so we graze our sheep on that. I am a carpenter as well and we have a turf bog also, so we get by. We have a good few foreign people here, they've bought a lot of land, Germans mostly, and they farm everything – cattle, sheep, goats, chickens and all that. They just use it for their own use to feed themselves.'

'There's an Irish college up the road,' said his wife, 'and students come here from Derry, Dublin and all over. We keep the students in our own home here for three weeks, to learn Irish. They meet the people in the area and you show them how to cut turf, how to save turf, how to bake, in Irish all the time. The ones that are homesick and cry the day they come, they cry the day they go home. They get so used to the people that they do not want to leave.'

I could well believe it. As well as the farmer and his wife there were a couple of friendly sons around who always seemed to be doing things for me, such as putting my bicycle away or fetching it out, for which I had to keep thanking them.

The Irish answer to 'Thank You' had just become 'No problem', the equivalent to *'Bitte Schön'* in German, *'De rien'* in France and 'Don't mention it' in America. It has now become universal in England, but at the time it was a surprise to find that if a man put a pint of Guinness down in front of me and I said 'Thank you', he would reply 'No problem'. There was a lot of 'Thank you' and 'No problem' in Croicsli.

Next day in heavy rain but with the wind on my back I struggled as far as Creeslough, where I stayed in a dingy B&B which I chose because it was opposite the pub so I had not far to go to find a television set. I was now myself infected with the World Cup fever which had swept the country, and this was the night of the first of Ireland's World Cup games. It was a famous victory, as Ireland beat Italy 1–0 by a goal scored early in the game. Thereafter the most popular bits were shots of Jackie Charlton (huge cheers) and of the Italian manager (roars of laughter).

The weather was in a most benevolent mood next day, smiling because of the victory over Italy. All was blue and green and brown, and peace and quiet, as I made my way to the well-hidden Doe Castle. In Donegal they don't really like you to know where anything is, so having taken the preliminary step of putting all the place names in Irish, in the case of somewhere like Doe Castle

190

they simply do not put up any signs at all, prefer-ring to pretend that it does not exist. By judicious enquiry I cracked the secret, which is that you turn left at the Post Office in Creeslough and you go about two miles down a little winding road. You then come upon Doe Castle in the form of a well-kept ruin with a moat on one side and the sea on three. It was built in the fifteenth century and given over to the McSweeneys, who were Scottish Galloways, otherwise mercenary soldiers brought over by Irish chieftains to assist them in fighting each other. There is a big round tower, with a modern plaque reading:

> Erected to the memory of Owen
> Second Papal Marquis McSweeney
> who died on 12th February 1986
> Proud descendent of the ancient and noble
>   house of Doe.
> On God's side were their souls.

The heavy iron gates of the castle were standing open and there was no sign of life anywhere, which made it slightly uncanny. I felt as if I were involved in a Hitchcock film and imagined a slam behind me as the gate crashed to and was locked. Then I would hurry round to the other gate where there would be another clash of metal and there I should be, mysteriously locked into a derelict castle by an invisible hand. Who would it be? A McSweeney ghost? My heir at law, wishing to accelerate his

191

inheritance? My wife's lover? MI6? Mossad? The possibilities were endless, but there was no such mysterious happening. All that actually occurred was that a fisherman arrived as I came out.

'How are the sea trout?' I asked.

'There's more to fishing than fish,' he replied cryptically, and strode off over the sands.

After Doe Castle I passed through Carrigart, which is quite a small place, but where the people were arriving at the Catholic church in droves. I counted more than fifty cars in the churchyard, forty more in the road, one bus, three minibuses, two tractors, sundry bicycles and a considerable host arriving on foot. There were young and old, male and female, hale and infirm, and between them illustrated the utter futility of trying to make this a Protestant country by penal laws, the plantation of Scotsmen, or any other means. The thought that their ancestors had to pay tithes to support the Protestant clergy made me cross even after this lapse of time.

I went on through wonderful country, pausing at Mulroy, between Carrigart and Milford, to admire a vista over Mulroy Bay which rivals the Ladies' View at Killarney but has not got a crowd of people looking at it. Then I got a place to stay in Rathmelton which was a great delight after yesterday's squalor because it was so clean and comfortable.

'Would you like a cup of tea?'

'Oh, I would, yes please.'

So it arrived as ever with a plate of sandwiches and a pile of biscuits.

'Thank you.'

'No problem.' Rathmelton is spelt like that in order to confuse, and the 'th' is silent so it is pronounced 'Ra-melton'. I used constantly to forget the names of Irish places because they are so strange. I had earlier set off for Dunfanaghy and within five minutes had forgotten where I was going. It is not that I was lost – I knew I was on the right road, but I did not know where it went because I found the name Dunfanaghy quite impossible to retain in my memory.

Rathmelton is an attractive town by Irish standards, built along one side of the River Swilly. It must have been quite a trading place at one time as there are some fine old warehouses on the river bank, and a particularly handsome stone Georgian house at the end, clearly the residence of a prosperous merchant. It is a Planters' Town, started early in the seventeenth century as part of the Plantation of Ulster.

From 1594, Hugh O'Neill, Earl of Tyrone, had been in open conflict with the English. In 1601 a Spanish army landed at Kinsale and Tyrone marched to join them, but the Irish were defeated by the English and the Spanish withdrew. Tyrone was given a free pardon, but in 1607 he and Hugh O'Donnell, Earl of Tyrconnel, who were faced with a steady decline in their influence and were also under suspicion of treason, sailed from Lough Swilly to Europe, abandoning Ireland forever. The Flight of the Earls, as it was known, left their estates to be confiscated and parcelled out among English and Scottish settlers. This, the Plantation of Ulster, by introducing Protestant settlers among a Catholic population, sowed the seeds of the conflict that has persisted in that part of the island up to the present time. T. B. Macaulay, historian, poet and statesman, speaking on the State of Ireland in the House of Commons in 1844, put it that 'no enmity that ever existed approaches in bitterness the mutual enmity felt by populations which are locally intermingled, but have never morally and politically amalgamated; and such were the Englishry and the Irishry'.

On the Republican side of the border this is all in the past.

Donegal, geographically speaking, is a part of Ulster though not, of course, of that part of Northern Ireland which is mysteriously referred to as 'The Province' and is part of the United Kingdom. Rathmelton is only a short step from Londonderry and is well sprinkled with Protestant churches of different denominations, but on this side of the border they live in harmony regardless of religion. So the owner of my B&B assured me, and said it was a mystery that they preferred to blow each other up on the east side of the border rather than live in peace as they did on the west. I couldn't help feeling that I would rather be an Irish citizen in Rathmelton than a British one in

194

Belfast, of whatever religious persuasion I might be. But as a superficial passer-through I should not really express my opinion.

The greater part of the next day I spent at, or getting to, or coming back from, Glenveagh, a castle in the National Park in a superb setting by Lough Veagh. It has a garden of over twenty acres, strong on fuchsias and rhododendrons, with fine trees and exotica, and a good line in statuary, both classical and oriental. The castle was built in 1861 by an evil man called John George Adair who evicted 244 tenants all at once to make room for his building and gardening ambitions. It then passed through several pairs of American hands and is now public property, and beautifully maintained. The rhododendrons are giving trouble as usual and at one point where the estate staff had set about clearing them, there was a notice:

> Sorry about the mess.
> We are clearing wild rhododendrons to protect the oakwoods and moorlands of Glenveagh.
> It will take ten years for the woods to recover after the rhodos are gone, but we think it is worth the wait.

Quite right too.

At Letterkenny where I was that evening, I had dinner with a judge to whom I had an introduction.

His name I will suppress as he put forward some political opinions and Irish judges are not supposed to have political opinions. He explained to me with compelling clarity that the last thing the Irish Government wanted was a United Ireland. 'It costs you people three billion pounds a year to police Northern Ireland, which is half our national budget, and there is no way we can afford it. We cannot even afford to police our own country properly, for they keep letting out of jail the people I send there. They let them out as an economy measure.'

Now this was a new thought to me, and when I got back to England I started to explain to people that all the talk from Mr Reynolds, who was then Prime Minister, about not being able to drop from the Irish Constitution the claim to the 'whole Island of Ireland', was just so much humbug. Any obstacles that he put in the way of a United Ireland were there for the very good reason that he did not want to be lumbered with it. As so often happens when I appear to speak with authority, I was entirely wrong. The peace process immediately took a great stride forward with Mr Reynolds of all people apparently making the running. I can only suppose that Mr Major and Sir Patrick Mayhew, the Northern Ireland Secretary, had somehow hit upon a tactic of hard-fought unconditional surrender which left Mr Reynolds out in front, like it or not.

I asked my friend the judge what it was like to sit on the bench in Donegal.

'If they were less economical with the truth it would be simpler for me to arrive at just and fair decisions.'

I protested at the words 'economical with the truth', a phrase introduced into the language by Lord Armstrong, whose cavalier attitude to veracity disgraced the British Civil Service. I thought that both he and his phrase should be expunged from our memories.

'Well, for good or ill it has passed into the English language, but if you prefer it the local term is "We won't lose our case for the want of a word." It has the same result in the end, so one watches their faces more intently than one listens to what they are saying.'

'Are you, a judge, saying that the greater part of the evidence is to be taken from the expression on the faces of the people in front of you, and not from what they say?'

'That is quite so. They have prepared what they are going to say but they are not all fantastic actors, though the ladies are generally better than the men. We on the bench are there to see fair play and do our best in conscience, and that is all we can do.' He explained that a free and easy attitude to the truth became ingrained on the Irish people because their Protestant landlords treated them so disgracefully that any weapon of defence was fair, perjury included. I accept this entirely, but it is an unfortunate legacy. I later read in a paper called *The Kerryman* that car insurance premiums in Ireland were twice as high as the next highest in Europe, and this is because if you lightly graze the bumper of an Irishman's car he is likely to be pushed into court in a wheelchair in a state of very great suffering. A substantial award of damages will often make him feel much better, if not send him dancing and jigging to the bank. As something similar happened to one Ernest Saunders, a swindler who got over Alzheimer's disease as soon as they let him out of jail, you cannot say that it is a wholly Irish phenomenon.

The judge was soon going to retire, at the age of 70, and talked of getting another job.

'Don't,' I said. 'Enjoy yourself instead.'

'Well, I was thinking of getting a job investigating fraud in the European Community.'

'Do!' I said hastily. 'I cannot think of a better man for the job.'

I hoped he would get it. It would not matter if all the proceedings were in a foreign language. He could just watch their faces intently without bothering about what they are saying.

Letterkenny was my last stop in Donegal, and I warmly recommend Donegal as a county. Anyone who has not been to Ireland before would be overwhelmed with delight at the beautiful mountains and moorland. If you have worked your way up by bicycle from further south like me, some of this is a combination of what you have seen before, but the barren Rosses and the determined

198

Irishness of the road signs and the specially
delightful people of Croicsli gave it a flavour of
its own, which I hope the march of progress has
left unspoilt.

DUBLIN

From Letterkenny I went to Dublin by bus, passing through the Debatable Land where the border crossing point was guarded by a huge military installation of metal and barbed wire. Having read all about bombs and shootings I expected to find Northern Ireland a bit frightening, but it was so completely placid that I fell asleep. When I woke up I was back in the Republic, among the familiar Irish Tourist Board Approved signs on the bed-and-breakfast places.

I went to Dublin for three reasons. I thought I might have misjudged it last time, when I had not much liked it; my tape recorder had now gone entirely over to Pinky and Perky mode, so something needed to be done; and I had promised to call on my friend Marie Louise. On all three counts the visit was a success.

The bicycle came with me on the bus, and on arrival there was a bit of dodgy cycling down Grafton Street to the Irish Tourist Board Office and some tricky map reading to find the B&B they booked for me at 'Sandymount Green past Reilly's pub in the house that is covered with ivy'. The owners of the ivy-covered house were full of useful talents. The landlady made me extremely comfortable, the landlord was a taxi-driver and took me to and from Marie Louise's house that evening, and the son was an engineer who showed me how to work the tape recorder which Marie Louise arranged for me to borrow. (I took the BBC one to the Dublin City University where the best brains in the Audio-Visual Department pronounced it to be incurably ill and lent me another.)

In the ivy house there were a lot of tall and friendly young men who were university students in digs, plus a couple of American girls who were in transit like me. I found myself vying with one of the girls to see who could outdo the other in praise of Doc Martens shoes. I had worn mine daily for cycling and walking and they were supremely comfortable for both purposes. The cobbler at home sold me liquid Nikwax to put on them and I think it made them waterproof. In heavy, continuous rain my feet ended up wet, but I think that was because my socks acted as a wick and conveyed the water to my feet, not because the shoes leaked.

I had telephoned Marie Louise from Letterkenny and she invited me to her house on the evening that I arrived in Dublin. She opened the front door with the words 'Hello, Howard's End', which was a reference to the deplorable joke I had made in the BBC studio where we met before. I am sorry if I tickle your curiosity, but over the joke itself a veil must be drawn. My late brother-in-law regarded me as a terrible prude, and one of his pleasures was to send me picture postcards of naked ladies from his frequent holidays abroad. He always maintained that the cards were tasteful and artistic, and as they both gave enjoyment to the postman and amused me, I did not mind. In general, though, I am very strait-laced with a strong dislike of vulgarity and profanity, and regard the above-mentioned joke as a most regrettable lapse.

It is ten years since I have seen Marie Louise, but I picture her as small, dark, lively and attractive, and if I said late-thirties in age I do not think she would object. She had laid on a bit of a party, and I spent an enjoyable evening in the company of some pleasant intelligent people who explained to me that not only could they not afford Northern Ireland, they positively did not want it. It was not so much that they did not wish to be lumbered with the likes of the Reverend Ian Paisley, though they did not, but they regarded Northern Ireland as the worst manifestation of the general backwardness of the British in respect of Europe.

They themselves had turned their backs on that part of history and embraced Europe with open arms, whereas they found going to Belfast like stepping back in time. Of course they were quite keen on that embracing business as the Irish had just wheedled some more money out of Jacques Delors, as a follow-up to the judicious bribes he sent their way when they were voting on the Maastricht Treaty. Even we might have embraced him on those terms.

There was a veterinary surgeon present (a 'vit', no less) who produced a new theory of sea trout. They employed, he said, organo-phosphorous insecticides to kill the lice on the salmon and poisoned the sea trout in the process. Also the seals kept breaking into the salmon cages so the lice-infested salmon escaped and infected the sea trout, which meant that the sea trout were losing both ways.

I realised next day that I had indeed misjudged Dublin on my first visit. It has, as I found by strolling about in the sunshine next day, a good number of fine buildings and a merciful paucity of very bad ones. I saw only one concrete office block all the time I was there. The jewel of the city is Trinity College, which is like a greatly expanded Cambridge College, each beautiful quadrangle succeeded by another equally beautiful. The effect was enhanced by its being vacation for all but the finalists, and perhaps if ten thousand students with holes in their jeans had been milling around the place, the effect might not have been so good. As it was, a group of young gentlemen in white were playing croquet in one quadrangle, a game which, at Trinity at least, is conducted in decorous silence and does not provoke shouting like tennis or swimming. On the cricket field there was no cricket,

but an elegant young man in a waistcoat was practising casting with a dry fly, so in spite of the Irish
being so bang up-to-date in respect of Europe,
Trinity appeared to be caught in a Victorian time
warp of gentleman-like occupations and good
behaviour.

The buildings, dating from the time of William
IV to that of Edward VII, harmonise beautifully
until you come to the Berkeley Library. This was
built more recently in a style they call 'Brutalism',
though 'Brutish' would be more like it. It spoils
the corner of an otherwise elegant quadrangle but
it gave me a high opinion of Henry Moore. The
Fellows had proposed to buy one of his sculptures
to put outside this library, but when he saw the
plans he said he would gladly give them a sculpture for nothing provided they put it anywhere
other than near that dreadful building. It reposes
in the second quadrangle on the sacred grass where
only Scholars and Fellows are allowed to tread,
and it looks very fine. With the money saved the
Fellows bought a sculpture suitable to the brutish
library which I later described to a sculptress who
I met as 'looking like a globe that has come under
artillery fire'.

'That will be a Pomodoro,' she said (or at least
it might have been Commodoro, but it was something like that). Evidently there is a man somewhere called Pomodoro or Commodoro who makes
a living by selling globes that have been shot up by
artillery.

The *Book of Kells* is kept in the Old Library at Trinity and viewing it is like paying one's respects to the embalmed corpse of Lenin. It lies in state in a sort of catafalque within a mausoleum, in company with the Book of Armagh and the Book of Dimma. You shuffle past it in a long queue and get told to move on by a KGB man if you try to linger. What you see, in the form of two illuminated pages, is very fine indeed. Outside Trinity there should be two big bronze statues, one of Edmund Burke and one of Oliver Goldsmith, both alumni of the college, but Goldsmith was missing. I found this very distressing as I regard him as one of the greatest models of written English, so I hoped nothing had happened to him.

'Where is Goldsmith?' I demanded of the college porter.

'He blew over.'

'What do you mean, "blew over"? He can't have blown over!'

'Well, he did. In a wind, and got damaged.'

'Just like that? Stood there for years and suddenly blew over?'

'Yes.'

'Unlikely!' I thought, and applied to the graduate girl who was gathering people together for a conducted tour.

'Well,' she said, 'it happened on Saint Patricks Day, and that is all I can say.'

Neither she nor the porter pretended that on 17 March there had been a hurricane the like of which you would not believe, which took all the tiles off the chapel roof and blew buses over in O'Connell Street, knocking Goldsmith over in the process. In default of a sworn statement to that effect I do not believe their story. I believe that, in the words of the eighteenth-century judge who dismissed the case against some young gentlemen of Trinity who unfortunately shot and killed their tutor, it was 'a student prank which got out of hand'. Boyish spirits are all very well, but I wish the young gentlemen would leave Goldsmith alone and content themselves with playing football with the Pomodoro globe.

I had arranged to meet Marie Louise at the famous Dublin tea shop and coffee house called Bewley's. The tip that I give anyone who is in Dublin and arranges to meet someone else at Bewley's is that there are three Bewleys'ses. Marie Louise waited at one and I at another until I got around to asking if there was more than one, as a result of which I arrived 20 minutes late at the right place to find a rather disgruntled Marie Louise at the entrance.

I really knew very little about Marie Louise, except that she was good company and an ex-perienced journalist. 'Networking' was not a word then in use, but her contacts were obviously wide-spread. It was she who had got me a replacement recording machine from the City University, and she showed me the proper interview technique for using it on people such as herself. It was she who had directed me to Willie Daley and the judge at Letterkenny, and come up with the name of Michael Delaney when she heard I was going to the Dingle Peninsula. Also, she was a fervent enthusiast for anything Irish. We talked about Willie Daley the matchmaker, who she said was the seventh son of a seventh son, and therefore had unusual powers. 'Clare, where he comes from, is full of bachelor farmers. Now Willie would tell you they are fine healthy men with lots of land but I know better!'

I knew a bit better too. Some of them are fresh men with a good head of hair, but getting on a bit all right and maybe hitting 80. Still, there are others.

She switched to the financial side of match-making. 'It is to do with dowry and with land. Land is much more important than people in Ireland. We spent so long fighting for it, the greatest plays have been written about it, people have died for land, people have killed for land, and the men would not leave the land. The women would go to work in England or America, so a lot of the places were left with the men still on the land. That is why European women and American women come to find husbands at Lisdoonvarna.'

I said that the small farmers that I had met eked out their living from the land with some other trade.

'I remember meeting a farmer in County Clare,'

she said. 'A big fat farmer on a brand new tractor on a mobile phone. Not only was he a farmer, he was also a gravedigger and an undertaker; he dug gardens; he cleaned the graves of families who were living abroad; he was also a boot-legger' (I think, unless she said 'brick-layer'); 'he was a handyman; he fixed gates; he shod horses; he told me that altogether he had ten jobs.'

We were sitting in Bewley's up to this point, which Marie Louise declared was 'one of the most famous coffee houses in the world'.

'One of the *three* most famous coffee houses in the world,' I insisted, in view of my recent experience, but she was right. This was the superior one in Grafton Street, founded by the Quaker family of Bewley and offering coffee, I suppose, as an alternative to strong drink. I think I was too much alarmed at having kept Marie Louise waiting to pay much attention to the outside, but the *Blue Guide* tells us that there is an 'Egyptian mosaic façade'. Inside you sit around in Edwardian surroundings on little chairs at little tables and the coffee is, of course, excellent. I notice also from the *Blue Guide* that I was right in another sense about one of the three most famous coffee houses. Bewley's, it says 'belongs with other famous survivals of European 'café society', the Café Greco in Rome and Paris Café Floré: it should not be missed.'

At this point we moved out into Grafton Street to stroll around. 'Dublin is really a village because it is very small and easy to get around,' said Marie Louise. 'It has fantastic theatre. It has great music – even on Grafton Street.' (I think she said 'even' on Grafton Street because it has smart shops and is more Piccadilly than Oxford Street. The pavements were fairly crowded with people doing their superior shopping in the superior shops, and it hardly seemed a likely place for busking.)

'Dublin is full of life and vigour,' she went on. 'It is a city in which you can never be lonely. Joyce was a Dubliner, Behan was a Dubliner. It has a wonderful pub culture of craic and music and song and dance and fun.

'It's very near the sea,' she said, going off on what seemed to me to be a tangent.

'What good is the sea to you?' I demanded. 'You can't swim in it, can you?'

'We've got some of the cleanest coasts in Europe,' (defiantly.)

'Aren't they *cold* and clean, like water out of a tap?'

'We are used to that,' (firmly, and not to be put off.) 'It is beautiful round the coast, round Dun Laoghaire and round Wicklow. It's five to ten minutes from the sea and it's five to ten minutes from the mountains so you have everything, for Dublin is nestling between the mountains and the sea.' Or, as you might say, cradled.

Now her enthusiasm burst into song:

Dublin can be heaven
With coffee at eleven
And a stroll round Stephen's Green
There's no need to hurry
There's no need to worry
You're a king, and the lady's a queen.

Well, she was right enough about Dublin, and you get a good class of street entertainer if you like that sort of thing. Generally I regard busking as a form of noise pollution and might give the buskers money to stop but certainly not to carry on. There was, however, a very good string trio in Grafton Street and further on a group who said they were called Is it Working?, which seems a good name for a group, unless they were talking about my recording machine, which I think perhaps they might have been. They were quite jolly to talk to, but when they broke into song they sang with false American accents like any other pop group, and I left them performing a melancholy piece of which the refrain was: 'What Went Wrong?'

Further on there was a street poet, whose offering 'written by myself' and which he insisted on reading into my machine, started thus:

I'd like to die still on duty with a verse on my lips,
A last great performance before I cash in my chips.

I've no wish for cremation or burial at sea
So pay close attention, for this is my plea: –
Bury me next to the only love I have known
Bury me I beg you by Molly Malone.

There were three more verses which I would describe as being of equal merit.

As the poet has brought Molly Malone upon the scene, I will tell you more about her. She was the girl who, in the song, wheeled her wheelbarrow through streets broad and narrow, crying 'Cockles and mussels, alive alive-o.' That was her day job. She was extremely pretty, and by night she turned to another, and older, profession, particularly among the young men of Trinity College. She died young in 1699 and in 1999 they put up a bronze statue of her at the bottom of Grafton Street, where she stands, complete with barrow.

Before I left I paid a further respectful visit to Trinity. The list of old members of the college is like a roll of honour of English literature, and includes Farquhar, Congreve, Swift, Burke, Thomas Moore, Oscar Wilde, J. M. Synge, Oliver Goldsmith, Nahum Tate, Bishop Berkeley and Samuel Beckett. I doubt if there is another institution in the British Isles or anywhere else in the world that can come near it, and it all goes to confirm my theory of the benefits of a childhood spent in speaking translated Irish instead of ordinary English.

There may be some who are not entirely

convinced by my theory, and I just say that there must be *some* explanation of the extraordinary gifts of the Irish nation in the use of the English language. They are more prolific in great writers than the Scots or the Welsh, and the same ability shows itself as much in the spoken word as in the written, because Irish political orators have always been every bit as talented as any who spoke English.

Possibly the greatest of them all was Richard Brinsley Sheridan, the author of the *School for Scandal*. Sheridan, who was a politician as well as a playwright and a theatre manager, played a major part in the impeachment of Warren Hastings, the first Governor-General of India. The first of his two speeches against Hastings was made in the House of Commons, and Macaulay says that 'the impression which it produced was such as has never been equalled. He sat down, not merely amidst cheering, but amidst the loud clapping of hands, in which the Lords below the bar and the strangers in the gallery joined. The excitement of the House was such that no speaker could obtain a hearing; and the debate was adjourned. Within four and twenty hours, Sheridan was offered a thousand pounds for the copyright of the speech, if he would himself correct it for the press. The impression made by this remarkable display of eloquence on severe and experienced critics, whose discernment may be supposed to have been quickened by emulation, was deep and permanent. Mr

Fox being asked by the late Lord Holland what was the best speech ever made in the House of Commons, assigned the first place without hesitation, to the great oration of Sheridan.' This was in the time of Pitt and the great Charles James Fox himself, when fine orators abounded.

Sheridan on his own proves nothing, but there have been many other brilliant Irish orators, such as Burke, Grattan, Parnell and O'Connell. The island has produced more of them than could reasonably be expected and eloquence seems to me to be a gift that Irish politicians still possess, on either side of the border. Flowery oratory is now out of fashion, but if you listen with attention to the spoken style of almost any Irish politician, you will be struck by the cogent clarity and even elegance with which the words are put together. In my case this includes the Reverend Ian Paisley. I may not always like what he says but I never fail to admire the way in which he says it.

For all this you are free to choose whatever explanation you prefer. You may like to say that it is the effect of breathing the Irish air, or of the Irish education system, or of drinking Guinness and eating potatoes. I do not think that you can say it is the Celtic blood, for if it was the writers and orators would have names like McSweeney and O'Brien, and they don't, or not many of them. I prefer to say that if you are surrounded from your earliest years by people speaking like those

in the Aran Islands (and that is certainly translated Irish) or like Willie Daley, it will rub off and
give you a delicate ear for words which stays with
you even if, like Sheridan, you are transplanted
to England and educated at Harrow.

KERRY AND CORK

The Dingle Peninsula, the Ring of Kerry, Glengarriff and home – that was the plan for the rest of the journey. Those who had been to the first two of these places had made me the subject of scorn and derision for having missed them on my earlier trip, and Glengarriff was very highly spoken of by W. M. Thackeray. I had not met anyone else who had been to Glengarriff, which was enough to make it seem that a visit might count as an exercise in exploring.

There is, or was, no difficulty in putting a bicycle on a bus in Ireland, and from Dublin to Limerick was a pleasant journey. Not so the bus ride from Limerick to Tralee, as I was shaken and rattled on a bouncy bus, with the noise of pop music dinning in my ears, accompanied by the sound of giggling teenagers. It was an unspeakable relief to reach the cool, quiet calm of the B&B outside the town that I had booked in advance for once, as I knew I should arrive quite late.

'Would you like a cooked breakfast?' asked my hostess, as always.

'Yes please.'

'You wouldn't rather have scrambled egg and smoked salmon?'

'Oh yes I would.'

So next morning the main feature of my breakfast was a piece of smoked salmon which covered the whole of the bottom of a large plate and was itself piled high with scrambled egg with bits of smoked salmon in it.

Tralee sits at the head of its own bay on the west coast, at the start of the Dingle Peninsula, and from Tralee I rode to the town of Dingle in a mist. There was no point in attempting the Connor Pass, which is the scenic route, as I should not have seen anything but mist, which is all that I saw on the route that I did take anyway. Dingle proved to be a trippery town, and Ireland lost their World Cup match 2–1 to Mexico that evening, so it was in rather a disappointed frame of mind that I set off next morning. Never mind, a visit to the Gallarus Oratory, a ride via Ballyferriter to call on Mr Michael Delaney, and then cycling on by Slea Head cured it all. I find that Ireland often has that effect. If you say to yourself that some part of it is disappointing, something happens to make you eat your words.

Thus it was that as the mist lifted next day after the Mexico match, my spirits lifted with it. I cycled uphill, puffing vigorously, from Dingle Bay to the Gallarus Oratory, a beautiful little building, measuring about seven yards across and shaped like an upside-down boat. It is one of the earliest ecclesiastical buildings in Ireland, dating from the seventh century and in spite of being thirteen hundred years old and made entirely of stones fitted together without the use of mortar, it is perfectly watertight. It is quite solitary and was never part of a community, but was either a place to which monks repaired to pray, or possibly where one or two lived as hermits. It looks out over the sea towards Ballyferriter and America, with a ring of hills behind. An American girl who was also visiting it gave me her map of the Dingle Peninsula, as she was leaving the next day and had finished with it. Someone had given it to her, she gave it to me, and I later gave it to another American girl, who was the one with whom I had discussed Doc Martens shoes in Dublin and who reappeared in a tea shop in Dingle.

At the start of this expedition I had been quite diffident about asking utter strangers to talk into my recording machine but I was used to it by now. Accordingly, I knocked boldly on the front door of Mr Michael Delaney, which I had been advised to do because he is an authority on all things Dingle. He showed no surprise but asked me in for tea. As everyone west of Dingle speaks Gaelic, he is not, of course, called Michael Delaney, this being merely a feeble English corruption of his true style and title which is something sounding like Mickhoil O'Doo-thlorn-ye. He is the local schoolteacher at a school outside Ballyferriter 'just over the hill here from us, which is the most westerly school in Europe'.

He explained to me that Ballyferriter means 'the town of the Ferriters', the Ferriters being a family that live around here, of Norman extraction who came via England from France in the thirteenth century. The most famous of the Ferriters was a man called Pieras Ferriter. He was the local chieftain and led a rebellion against the English and then fled to an island and hid in a cave. It was so small that he had to lie on his back and this is the verse that he wrote:

Oh God above, have you not pity on me
In my lonely prison, that I can scarcely see the
  day?
The drops of water from the roof fall on me
And all I can hear is the sound of the sea at
  my heels.

The above is the impromptu translation he gave of the verse he had previously recited in Irish and even allowing for some loss in translation it seemed to have some of the qualities of a verse of the Greek poetess Sappho, and certainly to be a great improvement on the street poet of Dublin.

The picture of Michael Delaney that I have in my mind is of the ideal primary school head teacher. That is to say, he said he was the teacher, and I have assumed that he was the head teacher, but if he wasn't he ought to be. He was neat and trim and quiet and knowledgeable in the extreme, and either he was actually surrounded by books, or else that is just my imagination, but again, if he wasn't he ought to have been. I would have entrusted to him any children that I happened to have with complete confidence, and he struck me also as a man who was happy with his lot.

He told me another Ferriter story in connection with a rock called Sybil Head, which you could see from his house; 'Sybil Head is a strange name and the rock is named for a lady who came from Galway. On one occasion the Ferriters went in their boats up to Galway and the chieftain of the Ferriters met the daughter of the local chieftain whose name was Lynch, and she was Sybil. The Ferriter chieftain wanted to marry her and bring her back home, but when they approached the father he would not agree. This did not deter the Ferriters, for the two of them eloped and fled back to their castle here. They lived happily there for a day or two, but one morning the chieftain woke up and saw that the whole bay was black with the boats of the Galway people. So to save his wife he brought her and hid her in a secret cave down on the cliff edge. Straight away then there was a fair battle between them and the Galway people were defeated, but afterwards when Pieras Ferriter went back to the cave to get his wife the tide had come in and drowned the lady. So that is Sybil Head, named after Sybil Lynch who was drowned.'

While stoutly defending Galway as a city of superior quality, Michael Delaney conceded that architecturally it wasn't up to much. 'Truly speaking most of our towns have just grown up by accident, higgledy-piggledy, and it is just in recent years that we have tried to build them up and make them nice.' I was more than anxious to meet him halfway and rejoined that the Irish towns are much cleaner than the English towns, and that there are practically no graffiti, both of which are true.

We thus began bandying compliments, I saying that the Irish were better behaved than us because they did not throw their litter around, and he that there were fewer of them, creating less litter to throw, and on this friendly note we parted.

I rode on towards Dingle, in a very satisfactory and happy frame of mind, as indeed I was so often on this trip. Near Slea Head I paused on a ledge above the grey-blue sea and gazed at the seven Blasket Islands spread out before me, the biggest being the Great Blasket. For me it was rather like being at Marathon or Thermopylae, one of the places I had read about and knew about, and which I get a thrill from visiting.

In this case it was because of that magnificent book *Twenty Years A-Growing*, which is the autobiography of Maurice O'Sullivan, only of course that was not his name at all; it was actually Muiris Ó'Suileabháin. 'I am a boy who was born and bred in the Great Blasket, a small truly Gaelic island which lies northwest of the coast of Kerry, where the storms of the sky and the wild sea beat without ceasing from end to end of the year and from generation to generation, against the wrinkled rocks which stand above the waves that wash in and out of the coves where the seals make their homes.' So he describes himself and his home. He was born in 1904, and later became a Peeler, otherwise a policeman. Although the times he describes are not all that remote, being less than a century ago, his account of life on the Great Blasket makes it seem like the Middle Ages. To give you more of a flavour, I will quote a passage from his boyhood, which refers incidentally to the Ferriters.

> Michael Baun was sitting shyly at the head of the table. All the night he had been looking at pretty Kate O'Shea. At that moment four boys arose to dance a set. They called four girls and Kate was one of them. I had a cat's eye on Michael, and Kate couldn't make a step to right or to left unknown to him. When the set was over, she sat down on the knees of Tomás-a-Phúncáin. Michael's eyes flashed. He gave three or four long sighs, stretched himself twice, and gave a yawn like one waking from sleep. Musha, upon my soul, said I in my own mind, the shafts of Cupid have pierced you, my boy.
> After a while Kate put her arm round

Tomás's neck. I was watching Michael. When he saw her he scratched his head and ground his teeth. Letting on nothing, I walked across to him and sat down on his knee.

'Michael,' said I, 'isn't it shy you are?'

'Faith, Maurice, there's no need for a person to leave his chair, when, if he did, he wouldn't get it again.'

'Listen, Michael, did you ever hear what Pierce Ferriter said one night when many people were gathered together, among them the girl who had won his heart, and he saw her sitting on the knee of another man?'

He looked at me sharply. 'What did he say?'

'This,' said I:

'A bitter sight it was to see,
Reclining on the knee of one
She loved, the woman who to me
Was dearest of all beneath the sun.'

He gave such a sigh that I felt myself going up into the air with the lifting power of it.

'Oh, Maurice, where did you hear that verse?'

'From my grandfather. Do you like it?'

'I like it well, for I know the way Pierce felt at that moment.'

'Anyone would think the same disease was on yourself.'

He bent his head, then raising it he looked across at Kate.

'That disease is on me, Maurice,' he said sadly.

The book was written in Irish and both the Irish original and the English translation were published in 1933. It supports my belief that English spoken in Ireland often amounts to Irish turned into English, for many of the O'Sullivan turns of phrase could well have come straight from the mouth of Willie Daley.

My two literary tips for anyone coming to Ireland are that they should get *The Aran Islands* of J. M. Synge and *Twenty Years A'Growing* by Maurice O'Sullivan. They both give the most vivid pictures of a way of life that is now extinct. The Great Blasket, which at one time supported about twenty families, is now deserted but remains a sight full of romantic interest for those who have read the book. Standing where the Spartans fell at Thermopylae you cannot think 'This is how Leonidas saw it' because the landscape has changed a lot, the sea having retreated since his time, but looking at the Great Blasket you can think 'This is just how Maurice O'Sullivan saw it.'

The Dingle Peninsula, like Donegal, has largely abandoned the English language. At one point I came across a big, important road sign written in bold letters on a yellow background which gave it an 'Ignore me at your peril' air. It said:

TAISTEAL
GO MALL

I had no idea what it meant, so whatever it was telling me to do, I could not do it.

Shortly afterwards I came upon a group of six small stone buildings which were, according to the notice, beehive tombs. They are like little Gallarus Oratories but shaped more like beehives than boats. They were on a farm and an old lady emerged from the house to demand one pound as a viewing fee.

'What *are* beehive tombs?' I asked.

'Houses for prehistoric monks.'

'There were no prehistoric monks.'

'Yes there were – over a thousand years ago.'

'That is later than Saint Patrick, and he was not prehistoric.'

At this she laughed heartily as if I were a droll fellow, but she clearly had no intention of changing her story which had earned her plenty of pounds in the past. I have not been able to find out any more about beehive tombs. The *Blue Guide* says they are 'curious primitive structures' and 'small stone shelters, shaped like a beehive', all of which you can see for yourself, but whether they were tombs or shelters, of what antiquity and for whose benefit, is not declared.

So I went bowling along through Dingle again, through Inch towards Castlemaine, the road flat, the sea calm on my right and with Slieve Mish above on my left. It was a long day which ended at an oasis outside Castlemaine where in a clean, spacious, well furnished B&B I was provided with an omelette, salad, pudding and a bath, the first bath I had had in four weeks, showers being the usual thing.

It was here that I had to take a decision, or face facts, or admit failure, as you please. I had started with every intention of riding round the Ring of Kerry as well as going to Glengarriff, as I have said. Anyone who cycles in Ireland at all seems to go round the Ring of Kerry. My daughter had done it and loved it. The map shows places with enticing names, such as Knockhadobar and Sneem. I could get round in two days and there was everything to be said for doing it except that I had cut it too fine: this was Tuesday, and my flight home from Shannon was booked for next Monday, so I had time for the Ring of Kerry or for Glengarriff, but not for both. Fool! But punctuality and the keeping to timetables is not to be expected in Ireland, and I had somehow frittered away, or otherwise lost, two days on this delightful trip. It could not be helped. I was particularly keen on Glengarriff, and there was a call I specially wanted to make on someone beyond Glengarriff at Union Hall, so the Ring of Kerry was sacrificed and remains well-ridden territory for almost every visiting cyclist in Ireland, except for me.

So, having decided that this was the way it had to be, next day I rode through Castlemaine aiming first of all towards Cork but turning at Poulgorm Bridge onto a minor road to Kenmare. It was very wet and very windy. I cursed the rain and the wind, but most of all I cursed the County Engineer of Kerry, as the ride from Poulgorm Bridge to Kenmare is potentially lovely and would be so but for his rotten roads. The Kerry County Engineer favours the bad-mosaic road surface to the exclusion of all others, and lets the roads get full of potholes as well. I can say with certainty that all the roads from Donegal southwards are better than the roads in Kerry, and Kerry is the first county I encountered where cyclists are condemned to jiggle and rattle on rotten roads. I was too wet and generally ground down when I reached Kenmare to do anything more than eat fish chowder in a pub and go to sleep.

Next morning I found the 'Save the Sea Trout' signs had reappeared, and got the definitive explanation from a man who runs a fishing tackle shop. 'The problems started when the government allowed fish farms to be set up in the estuaries and bays. The fish are mainly salmon, though they have rainbows and steelheads as well. Every angler knows that you have a background level of lice, and a fresh fish in from the sea is fresh because he has still got lice with the tails attached to them on the fish. But there has been an explosion of lice on the fish farms. The lice have fastened onto the millions of salmon inside these cages and each louse sends out up to forty thousand eggs and they drift on the tide and attach themselves to the sea trout in the estuaries. They are in such number that they damage the bodies of the sea trout, and our first, second and third year finnocks have been dying.' I cannot find the word 'finnock' in the dictionary, but that is what it sounded like.

The salmon farmers had been trying to deal with the lice by throwing insecticide into the open sea 'which damages the spats for the shellfish.' Furthermore 'not only are the sea trout dying but the salmon numbers are down as well for the salmon smoults have to run through these clouds of sea lice before they can get out to the open sea, and we are afraid they are dying on the way out to the feeding ground in Greenland and the Faroes.' He said there was a solution, which was to move the salmon farms at least twenty-five kilometres from the estuaries, as the lice would not be carried so far, but 'we are led to believe it would be more expensive because you need stronger cages out in the open water'.

The man who told me all this had, he said, 'a good broad Kerry accent. When I go to London a lot of people think I am a Dutchman.' This is something I should not have thought in London or elsewhere, but I had only recently become aware of the great variety in the Irish brogue. By bicycle you go so slowly from one part to the next that you may not notice the change, but it strikes you forcibly when you go, as I did, by bus from the fairly soft-spoken Donegal accent to the strange nasal whine of Dublin, and then quickly back to the semi-Dutchmen of Kerry.

From Kenmare I rode to Glengarriff, a mere 18 miles but the road goes up steeply and steeply down. My ancient guidebook says 'the road is splendidly engineered and can be climbed in top gear either way'. Not by me it cannot, but perhaps they meant in an Austin Seven. The lower slopes are very fine beside the River Sheen, which is rocky and has spectacular cataracts and torrents. I have no doubt that the upper reaches would have been fine also, if only I could have seen them through the mist. I stopped at a shop 11 miles from Glengarriff, by now in heavy rain, and they said it was up four more miles 'and then you will have a grand run down'. Up it was, and wet it was, and windy. You go through three tunnels at the top and I paused at the last one to make a BBC wildtrack of Irish rain, which they did not use as it sounded the same as any other rain. From the mouth of the third tunnel onwards you are supposed to be enjoying 'a profusion of wildly beautiful prospects' but fog and rain was all the prospect I could see on the grand run down, during which my waterproof became waterproof no longer and I got drenched to the skin and cold to the marrow.

No words of praise or thanks can be too high for Caseys Hotel in Glengarriff where a motherly lady, who did not seem to mind my dripping water all over the place, took me in, called me a 'poor lamb', pulled the cycling gloves off my frozen fingers, gave me a luxurious room and carried off my wet clothes to the boiler-house. The waiter put my bicycle in a shed and brought me tea and chicken sandwiches in front of a blazing fire in the lounge, saying he knew how enjoyable it was to sit by an open hearth in such circumstances as he had often been soaked and frozen as a Boy Scout.

The point to Glengarriff is that, like some parts of the west coast of Scotland, it is washed by the Gulf Stream and so never gets cold but abounds in tropical vegetation. Thackeray said of it: 'Were such a bay lying upon English shores it would be a world's wonder. Perhaps if it were on the Mediterranean or Baltic, English travellers would flock to it by hundreds.' I spent the next morning peering anxiously out at it from Caseys Hotel where I was pinned down by the Irish monsoon. In the afternoon it reduced itself to ordinary rain so I ventured out to admire the palms and bamboos in the public park and to climb up among rocks and hedges and trees to Lady Bantry's Lookout, where you get a panoramic view, in my case of fog. On getting back I was able to help an American girl who could not understand why her hired bicycle would not work. I fixed it in two seconds. All she had done was twist the handlebars through 180 degrees so the wheel was back to front, and all I did was to turn it round again.

I agreed with my motherly friend at Caseys Hotel that I would stay another night in the hope of better weather for visiting Garnish Island, which is sometimes given an extra i and called Garinish, and by either name is the jewel of Glengarriff. This was a wise decision as next day everything was sparkling and fresh in bright sunshine. The first boat leaves for the island at ten o'clock, so at ten o'clock sharp I was at the landing stage and, there being no other passengers, travelled out in solitary state.

The boatman told me that 'Garnish Island is actually the Latin name for it. The proper name for the island is Ilnacullin. The man who owned the island and started off the development on it employed an Italian architect and that is where the word Garnish came from, for the Italian architect brought that word into it, which would be about ninety years ago. The man's name that owned the island was Bryce, and it was the English War Ministry that he bought it from, and he was an English MP. The Gulf Stream flows into the harbour here at Glengarriff and it generates a heat on its own, but they built a shelter belt around the island which made it more like an oven. It contains the heat and you have plants and shrubs from all over the world growing there.'

Now that was an exciting prospect, and there was excitement in plenty on the way because to my astonishment there were a great many seals basking on the rocks in the harbour. I had never before seen seals in a state of nature, so the boatman took me to within about ten yards of some of them to have a look. On the whole they just looked at us, and perhaps flopped about a bit at our approach, but one colony jumped into the water and gazed at us with their eyes and whiskered noses just peeping out, regarding us with calm benevolence. It seems that the warmth of the Gulf Stream brings in the fish, and the seals follow the fish.

Whether the boatman was right in his etymology for the name Garnish I cannot say, and I fear he was wrong in saying that Harold Peto who designed the garden was an Italian, but he was right enough in his description of the garden itself. It is magnificent, but you need to be a bit more of a garden buff than I am to appreciate the technicalities. It was all very well for the guidebook to tell me that *Acacia Pravissima* grows as comfortably here as in its native New South Wales, but there were no labels on the plants so I did not discover which it was, and could not give it the kindly greeting that I reserve for visitors from the Antipodes. All the same I was quite content to wander about feasting my eyes on the lush colours, listening to the thrushes singing, and admiring the ornate Italian garden most of all. After a time some proper garden enthusiasts arrived, several of whom began taking close-up photographs of exotic blooms, which is the proper way to behave in such surroundings.

There is a Martello tower, otherwise a small round fort, which was built during the Napoleonic Wars. The island occupies a strategic position at the head of Bantry Bay and in 1796 the French were persuaded by the Irish republican patriot Wolfe Tone to send a force of fourteen thousand men to invade Ireland. The *Indomptable* with Wolfe Tone on board lay in Bantry Bay for six days. Wolfe Tone wrote in his diary; 'It is the dreadful stormy weather and easterly winds which have been blowing furiously and without intermission since we made Bantry Bay that have ruined us. Well, England has not had such an escape since the Spanish Armada; and that expedition, like ours, was defeated by the weather.' After the 1796 venture had miscarried, General Humbert made his further attempt to support an Irish rebellion and Wolfe Tone again arrived, to be captured at Lough Swilly, tried by court marshall at Dublin, and sentenced to death. He was refused execution by firing squad, attempted to cut his own throat and died a week later. The English would have hanged him, cut throat and all, if a legal process concerning the legality of his conviction had not kept them at bay. All of this activity explains why the English Government thought it necessary to fortify Ilnacullin, otherwise Garnish, commonly known as Garinish, and how it came to belong to the War Ministry before Mr Bryce acquired it.

It was after midday when I got back. By this time in the holiday I was very much fitter and only a month older than when I arrived in Ireland, so I had no qualms about setting off for Union Hall, a trip of some fifty miles. The sun shone, I pedalled along as blithe as a bird, and did the trip in an afternoon with no trouble at all, except for a brief period when an elderly Welshman decided to keep me company. His idea of enlivening the journey was to repeat some comical verses that he had made up about cycling, and I had to keep exclaiming at his wit and cleverness. I shook him off finally by stopping to buy some sandwiches and insisting upon eating them there and then. He had to go on, as he had already had his lunch. The sea was on my right as far as Bantry, then the road crossed moorland to Skibbereen. This is a niceish sort of town with a good sort of name (Irish towns ought always to have names like Skibbereen) set in Somerville and Ross country, by which I mean that the authors of the *Irish R.M.* stories lived nearby.

Thackeray arrived in Skibbereen on a Saturday, spent the night at the hotel, and on Sunday morning went searching for his breakfast:

And now the pangs of hunger beginning to make themselves felt, it became necessary for your humble servant (after making several useless applications to a bell, which properly declined to work on Sundays) to make a personal descent to the inn-kitchen, where was not a bad study for a painter. It was a huge room, with a peat fire burning, and a staircase walking up one side of it, on which stair was a damsel in a partial though by no means picturesque dishabille. The cook had just come in with a great frothing pail of milk, and sat with her arms folded; the hostler's boy sat dangling his legs from the table, the hostler was dandling a noble little boy of a year old, at whom Mrs Cook likewise grinned delighted. Here, too, sat Mr Dan, the waiter; and no wonder the breakfast was delayed, for all three of these worthy domestics seemed delighted with the infant.

He was handed over to the gentleman's arms for the space of thirty seconds; the gentleman being the father of a family, and of course an amateur.

'Say Dan for the gentleman,' says the delighted Cook.

'Dada, says the baby; at which the assembly grinned with joy: and Dan promised I should have my breakfast 'in a hurry.'

But for all the wonderful things to be seen in Skibbereen, Dan's pantry is the most wonderful – every article within is a makeshift, and has been ingeniously perverted from its original destination. Here lie bread, blacking, fresh-butter, tallow-candles, dirty knives-all in the same cigar box, with snuff, milk, cold bacon, brown-sugar, broken tea-cups, and bits of soap. No pen can describe that establishment, as no English imagination could have conceived it.

I did not stay at Skibbereen but went on to establish myself in a room not far from Union Hall, on a little inlet on the south coast.

I was going there for a purpose. At Union Hall I knew a man who was acting out a fantasy, which can be a very good thing to do as Peter Mayle discovered, he being the author of *A Year in Provence*. It is every man's fantasy to throw up the job he hates and go to live in a beautiful farm-house in sunny France where superb food and wine are always on tap and comic Frenchman provide light relief and innocent amusement. When Peter Mayle put all this in a book, all the people who dreamt of throwing up the jobs they hated and going to gorge and swill for evermore in perpetual sunshine, bought the book by tens of thousands, so it was a great success. Likewise, up to a point, my neighbour's son had dreamt of abandoning the job in computers at which he earned a huge amount but which he heartily hated, and taking his wife to run a pub in Ireland. Being a man of action he had not just dreamed, but had done it, and was now several months into this escapade.

Anyone else nurturing a similar fantasy could at that time have gone to Union Hall and asked for the pub that is run by an Englishman. It is a beautiful place, reached by a bridge across the harbour, so you would not have regretted the detour and whatever else might have been going on, there was certainly not a rat race. I arrived unannounced and unexpected. John was watching football on television in the empty bar, his wife was occupied with their daughter behind the scenes. By the time I had drunk two pints of Guinness and eaten a plate of chilli con carne things had livened up to the extent of two more visitors, this time girls from America, one of whom was his wife's cousin. As I left, two young Dutchmen turned up to ask where they could camp. Possibly the sleepy village might have been going to disgorge a couple of locals to lean on the bar later, and as an antidote to the cut and thrust of the computer world nothing could have been greater.

I did not talk to John directly about this dream which he had pursued. Spending one's days in an empty bar was not, to my mind, an idyllic existence, and possibly things had not worked out exactly as he expected. If this was so, it was not for me to bring the thought into the open, and anyway I might only have had such an idea because it had been suggested by my neighbour, his father, who thought that the whole undertaking was crazy. Crazy or not, it was a brave enterprise, and fortune favours the brave. I am not sure exactly what happened afterwards, but I think that someone may have established a yacht marina at Union Hall and so changed the place altogether. Certainly John was somehow swept up on the rising tide of Irish prosperity, sold up at an advantage, and now lives elsewhere, but I think nearby, in a state of tranquil prosperity – or so I believe.

After my visit to John, the trip was almost complete. What remained to be done was to get myself to Shannon from where I was to fly home on the following day. I had cut it a bit fine, but not too fine. I needed to get to Cork that evening, then to get a train from Cork to Limerick next morning, and after that to ride on from Limerick to Shannon.

Away I went, the sun still holding out and myself brimful of confidence. This was perfectly justified as I did the fifty miles to Cork with no trouble at all, but it was an uneventful ride and dull enough by comparison with the spectacular scenery I had got used to on the west coast. I spent the night in Cork, which I did not have time to explore, but thinking that I ought, before I left, to hear some of the traditional Irish music that was advertised by placards outside pubs everywhere, I found a place where some of it was going on. There were two fiddles, one played by a greybeard and one by a girl with a ring in her nose, plus a man with a guitar, and they played jigs relentlessly. They were tucked away in the corner and apart from me nobody took the least notice of them, neither stopping their conversation when they played nor applauding when they stopped. Of course, I made a wildtrack of them for the BBC, and, of course, the BBC did not use it.

Sitting in the bar and thinking back, I could see that the Dingle Peninsula is very fine as long as the mist is not too thick, and I was pleased with Glengarriff. All the same, as I pondered I realised that the further north I had been the better I had liked it. From Achill Island and beyond, through Mayo, Sligo and Donegal, almost everyone but me was Irish. Except where Greimann Reisen had tipped a busload out to view the grave of Yeats, tourists were rarely to be seen and such as there were, were all right. I rather liked the excitable Frenchman at Dulough Pass, and I got some amusement from the excitable Italians at Streedagh; as for the American girl at Lissadell, she had such lovely eyes that I was quite bowled over and delighted to make her acquaintance. From all of which I concluded that you get a good class of tourist north of Achill Island, if you get tourists at all.

Anyway, I loved it. I loved the beauty of the country and I loved the colourful friendliness of the people. I hope that in this book I have managed to let the people speak for themselves to an adequate degree, but I fear I have not done justice to the country. To borrow again from Madame de Bovet 'the pen,' she says, 'gets tired of describing landscapes of ever-varying line and light and colour, to which it can only apply a limited and monotonous vocabulary.' Which is why I have spared you any attempts at fine writing, in which I should inevitably fail.

Cork was really the end of the expedition. Next day I crossed the road from my B&B to the railway station and took a train to Limerick. Between Limerick and Shannon I paused to look at Bunratty Castle, but it is overdeveloped with a 'Folk Park', which is the sort of thing I do not like so I did not stay long. More evocative was the turning to Quin, down which I had gone at the very start of the trip. An enormous amount seemed to have happened in the month between, and I had, in the course of it all, formed a new opinion of Ireland.

I have from time to time made comparisons between Ireland and Greece, and I am not the first to have done so. Mr Piehler, who by now I regarded as an old friend as his book had come with me from start to finish, says of Connemara that its 'austere beauty can be matched only in Greece'. I had similar thoughts, but I also had them about the people themselves, and I had them in particular because both Greece and Ireland are devout nations full of devout people. The philosopher David Hume, although he was, I believe, of an atheistical turn of mind, said, 'Look out for a people entirely devoid of religion; if you find them at all, be assured they are but a few degrees from brutes.' There is no danger of that in Ireland or in Greece. If I travel in a Greek bus among women who cross themselves at every roadside shrine, I feel I am in good company, and I had the same feeling throughout the west of Ireland, especially at Carrigart, where a huge congregation was assembling for church on Sunday.

However, what I now consider to be the most striking aspect of the comparison is the way that the two countries have been transformed before my eyes as a result of their joining the European Common Market (as it then was). The change in prosperity of them both is astonishing. All over Greece you see public works being carried out by courtesy of the EU, and everywhere you see new houses springing up as a result of the widespread wealth which has flowed from their membership of that organisation. Ireland has boomed likewise, but more so, and the Irish are now richer per head than we are in England, or so I read. I had seen it all beginning to happen.

My own view of the EU is that it is a splendid organisation. They say it has stopped the French and Germans from fighting each other, and that alone is more than enough to justify its existence. My one wish is that we did not belong to it. The French and the Germans would not have fought each other if we had not joined, and so as far as that goes, we need not have bothered. Otherwise it seems to cost us a lot of money for very little benefit and I think we would have done better to stay out, like the Norwegians. These are contentious issues, and I introduce them only to say that one of the few aspects of the EU which reconciles me in some degree to our membership, is the way it has siphoned money out of our pockets and funnelled it into those of the Irish. This couldn't happen to nicer people, and when one considers how we treated them over the centuries when we had them in our clutches, I feel we owe it to them, so I am pleased.

I have heard it said that all this money is doing harm to Ireland, by making people hurry to accumulate the stuff in a way they never did before. Perhaps, but someone recently carried out a survey to see which countries enjoy the best quality of life. I don't know what countries were in the survey or how they were assessed, but I believe the United Kingdom came out as number twenty-eight. Ireland came out as number one, the best, and from my own experience I can truly say that I am not a bit surprised.

BIBLIOGRAPHY

Bartlett, W. H., *Scenery and Antiquities of Ireland*, George Virtue, London, 1841

Beckett, J. C., *The Making of Modern Ireland*, Faber and Faber, London, 1966

Black's Picturesque Tourist of Ireland (sic), 16th edition, A&C Black, Edinburgh, 1879

Blue Guide – Ireland, A&C Black, Edinburgh, 1998

Cobbett, William, 'Letter of 1834', in *Not by Bullets and Bayonets*, Molly Townsend, Sheed and Ward, London, 1983

de Bovet, Marie Anne, *Three Months Tour in Ireland*, Chapman and Hall, London, 1891

de Vere Hunt, Captain Vere, *England's Horses for Peace and War*, Bemrose and Sons, London, 1874

Dunlop, Robert, *Ireland from the Earliest Times to the Present Day*, OUP, Oxford, 1922

Handbook for Ireland, John Murray, London, 1864

Large, E. C., *The Advance of the Fungi*, Jonathan Cape, London, 1940

Ludlow, General Edmund, *The Memoirs*, Clarendon Press, Oxford, 1894

Macaulay, T. B., *The Works of Lord Macaulay*, Longmans, Green and Co, London, 1875

O'Connor, W. A., *History of the Irish People*, 2nd edition, Heywood, 1886

O'Sullivan, Maurice, *Twenty Years A-Growing*, OUP, Oxford, 1953

Piehler, H. A., *Ireland for Everyman*, J. M. Dent and Sons, London, 1938

Smith, Sydney, *The Works of Sydney Smith*, 4th edition, Longmans, Green and Co, London, 1848

Surtees, R. S., *Mr Sponge's Sporting Tour*, Bradbury, Agnew and Co, London, c1854

Synge, J. M., *Four Plays and The Aran Islands*, OUP, Oxford, 1962

Thackeray, W. M., *The Irish Sketch-book*, Smith, Elder and Co, London, 1865

Young, Arthur, *Tour in Ireland*, The Blackstaff Press, London, 1983